INDIA

Secrets of the Tiger

Managing Editor: Ruth Urbom

Project Editor: Christina Czapiewska

Editorial Assistant: Emma Agyemang

Creative Director: Alexander Rose

Jacket Design: Daniel Oliver

Design Layout: Vikram Parashar

Art Editor: David Fraser

Production Manager: Carol Titchener

Sales & Editorial Manager: Karen Lomax

Author: Paul Stump

Additional Material: Kaspa Hazlewood

ISBN 13: 978-0-7607-9232-2

ISBN 10: 0-7607-9232-1

A catalog record for this title is available from the Library of Congress

Printed and bound in Singapore

10 9 8 7 6 5 4 3 2 1

INDIA
SECRETS OF THE TIGER

Paul Stump

k

Kandour Ltd

Contents

Introduction

Left: Taj Mahal at dawn.

Like the tiger, its national symbol, India is fascinating and exotic.

The nation we know as India today, with its population of over a billion people, has existed in its present form for less than a century. But the diversity of India's people, geography, languages, and culture show that its history stretches far back in time. It is a history of conquering emperors, wealthy kingdoms, and but also of learning and culture. India is recognized as the birthplace of some of the world's great religions. Religion also plays an important part in daily life in India today, and it continues to attract visitors on their own spiritual journeys.

In past centuries, India's valuable spices and natural mineral wealth made it attractive to traders from other lands. Indian princes and kings lived rich, opulent lifestyles.

India is also a land of dazzling natural beauty. From the mighty Himalayas in the north, through the plains of Punjab, over to the hills of Assam in the east, and down to the tropical coastline of the south, India offers an amazing variety of landscapes, climates, flora and fauna.

And everywhere, there are the people of India. It is India's people who preserve its important cultural traditions and drive its technological and economic progress.

This book celebrates the people of India and the intriguing diversity of their country.

Patchwork

Left: One of the many colorfully embroidered Indian quilts.

Bottom Right: Vibrant flowers soaked in saffron water.

The colors of India's landscape are reflected in its celebrated tradition of embroidery and patchwork.

Most Indian regions have an individual and distinctive tradition of this craftwork. Punjab has traditional appliqué work called *Phulkari*, which is most often seen in the production of shawls and *chunnis*, or long scarves.

In Andhra Pradesh, Banjara women wear blouses and headscarves decorated with appliqué and mirror work. Rajasthan boasts an appliqué technique known as *gota* work. The region of Shekhawati is an important center for this technique.

Utility items like bags, lampshades, and placemats are also decorated using this ingenious method. Patchwork and embroidery are often the provinces of poorly paid craftswomen whose knowledge of centuries-old tradition is the only source of income for their families.

As one Indian academic puts it, "with a simple, inexpensive, environmentally friendly needle, palm leaf, spindle or loom, and the inherent skill of her hands, a woman can both support her family and enrich the national economy and export trade."

Embroidered quilts and patchwork have massive cultural significance beyond their everyday usage. Their motif and color, as in most Indian craft objects—however utilitarian—have deep significance that is rooted in religious and local traditions. The vivid range of local imagery influences all manner of textiles—garments, soft furnishings, and other items.

Bright pigments like these form the base for many dyes used in textiles.

Embroidery

The craft of embroidery has been developed and refined into a fine folk art in the various regions across India. Despite the influence of machine-made clothing and textiles, hand embroidery retains a strong presence across India, particularly in rural villages.

Many local traditions emphasize imagery from local flora and fauna, and geometric elements are also commonly seen. Birds, elephants, lotus flowers, apple blossoms, saffron flowers, and trailing vines may all be seen in Indian embroidery.

Materials as diverse as leather, silk, and velvet may be used as the base for precious embroidery work, but even simple cotton fabric can be embellished with colorful motifs. Extra texture and interest can be added with mica pieces or tiny mirrors sewn on with buttonhole stitches.

Indian brides will traditionally have at least a couple of elaborately embroidered saris in their wedding trousseau. Embroidered household textiles also have a long tradition in India, and have long been popular export items in the West.

Far Left: A vivid example of India's intricate embroidered fabrics.
Center: The art of Henna is typically applied to hands, where the pigment can last for days.
Left: This distressed diamond pattern is common in Indian arts and crafts.

Clothing often has specific religious meaning within India. These fabrics are an example of items offered to certain Hindu goddesses.

Diversity

Temples

Left: An elephant draped in colorful traditional cloth outside the Brihadisvara Temple in Tanjore.

Bottom Right: This ornate arcade demonstrates the art and precision of Indian religious architecture.

If there are many religions in India, it is fair to say that the followers of those faiths have erected more temples than anyone could count.

They are everywhere. In some cases, they present sights to the traveler that he or she is unlikely ever to forget. There are modern temples such as the ornamental marble Pilani Birla Mandir in the Rajasthan university town of Pilani. There are ancient ones, the 1600-year-old, biscuit-colored ruin of Dwarka in Gujarat, for example. There are small temples, like the tiny ones guarded by huge, humanoid statues deep in the jungles of Tamil Nadu. And there are vast, grand structures meant to impress pilgrims and visitors alike, such as the Golden Temple in Amritsar. This is the home of the Sikh faith, and not only is it one of

India's greatest temples, but it is also one of the most photographed and best-known religious buildings in the world.

Most of India's religions have built shrines over the centuries. Often these have been on a progressively larger scale, depending on the wishes of the senior religious figures, a kingly whim, or the circumstances of the time. Famine, for example, could wipe out the workforce. There could be shortages of raw materials. A conquering army could bring with it a new architectural style and rebuild what had already been started.

To list the glories of Indian temples would fill several books larger than this one—even without illustrations. Without exception, though, India's temples are magnificent works of architecture,

Diversity

often built swiftly by thousands of laborers and craftsmen. Almost all Indian temples are renowned for their artistic integrity, even at their most ornate. Few are more dazzling in this regard than the huge tower-like Meenakshi Sundareswar temple in Tamil Nadu, with each of its tens of thousands of stones like a living art gallery in itself. That this structure was once razed to the ground by war, and then rebuilt by the local Madurai Nayak rulers, is little short of phenomenal.

One of the most remarkable things about so many ancient temples is that they have survived for so long. India has often suffered religious turmoil, yet many of the most imposing statements of faith in the country—the temples—withstood the struggles and remained proudly on the skyline. It is hard to know whether this is because opposing faiths respected the shrines of others, or

whether the grandest temples were so well built they were practically impossible to demolish.

The architectural styles of Indian temples vary from tower-like structures, more common in the south of the country, to the dominant domes in the north. Towers are usually associated with lands further to the east of India. Indeed the Mamallapuram (Mahabalipuram), near Madras on the Indian Ocean, is, apart from its monolithic sculptures, home to a pagoda-like shore temple. There is only one surviving pagoda of what was once known as the Seven Pagodas. Six of them now lie submerged by the encroaching sea. Pagodas are definitely not what one would associate with India.

Scholars are divided on whether the dome in northern India shows influences of Persian and Muslim mosque-builders. The Moguls, who swept through the north in the 15th and 16th

Bottom Left: One of the many religious frescos that are part of the temples of India.

Center: An intricate Hindu religious sculpture from the Rajendra Cholan temple in southern India.

Right: A stone carving depicting symbolic animals typical to any shrine or temple.

Diversity

centuries, were great builders, and it is hard to believe they did not influence many native architects. But, at the same time, among the great glories of the cupola, or dome structure, characteristic of Moguls, is the gigantic 81-ton cupola topping the Brahadeeswara Temple at Thanjavur. This belongs to a much earlier period in the 10th century, called the Chola period. It was constructed by Raja Raja Chola, whose laborers are said to have pushed the dome into place using an inclined, four-mile-long (6.4 km) plane. The Chola architects behind this remarkable building also ingeniously ensured that the cupola, large though it is, never casts a shadow on the ground. The grandest of Muslim mosques in India is the Adina Mosque at Pandua, one of the capitals of the old Bengali Sultanate of the 14th and 15th centuries. Its carvings are known throughout the world, as are those of the Jama Masjid, or White Marble Mosque, at Ajmer.

There can be little doubt that religious strife did cost India some architectural jewels, with materials from one demolished mosque or temple being used to build another. But the fact that anyone gazing at these buildings can draw parallels between styles says much for the way India's religious diversity has managed to survive. One only has to look at the motif inscriptions of the ancient Jain and Hindu religions—the lotus and the chakra, for example—inside the vast mosques of Ahmedabad, Champaner, and Surat in Gujarat state to see how true that is.

Far Left: The astounding Vishwanath Temple in Khajuraho.
Left: Sun Wheel carving at the temple in Konark.

Moguls

The great Mogul Empire of India was led by descendants of Tamburlaine the Great, the Central Asian warlord who so terrorized the region in the 14th century. The great-grandson of Tamburlaine, Babar—who was a descendant of none other than Genghis Khan—went to India in 1526 at the request of an Indian governor. The governor needed help fighting a local war, but Babar became ruler, if only until 1530. His son Humayun succeeded him, and Humayun's son Akbar succeeded his father. Akbar was a mighty warrior, and rightly earned himself the title "the Great." The wise and compassionate Akbar was a Muslim, but he was a tolerant ruler. Although he expanded his empire to Kabul and Kashmir in the north and to Bengal in the east, he was an enlightened man. He tried to start a new faith, Din-i-Ilahi, an attempt to blend Islam with Hinduism, Christianity, Jainism, and other faiths. He actively celebrated Hindu religious festivals, such as Diwali. Under his rule, roads and waterways were built, and some of the most beautiful examples of Indian architecture—a tradition that would flourish under the Moguls—began to appear.

Babar Khan had established beautiful gardens in Kabul, Lahore, and Agra, and Akbar's son, Jahangir, continued his family's interest in gardens. He also promoted painting of the richest and most elaborate kind. It was Jahangir's marriage to the Persian princess Nur Jahan, or "Light of the World," in 1611 that brought Persian influence to bear on all aspects of Indian life. Shortly after Jahangir's death in October 1627, his son, Shah Jahan, succeeded to the throne. He inherited a vast and rich empire, and the mid 1600s probably marked the height of India's preeminence in painting and architecture. The Taj Mahal, rising like a swan from its surroundings, is perhaps the finest example of his influence, and it remains an icon 400 years after being built.

Bottom Left and Center: Two examples of the many colorful marble cenotaphs found in Rajasthan.

Right: The unmistakable Taj Mahal, perhaps the most important symbol of India.

Forts and Palaces

India's history has often been one of fierce conflict and invasion—but also one of fabulous wealth and royal splendor. Little wonder, then, that the country still boasts so many extraordinary demonstrations of both these elements of history. Its forts, moated and well-situated, with mighty, rugged walls, were and are the equal of any fort in the world. They are still spread across the country, many of them in a fine state of preservation. The same goes for the palaces, those pavilions to the majesty and reckless extravagance of its rulers. Two of India's most characteristic buildings are the Red Fort in Delhi and the Taj Mahal in neighboring Agra—perhaps *the* symbol of India. Their fame demonstrates just how important a part of the Indian environment these buildings were, and still are today.

The construction of forts resulted not only from defending India against foreign invaders, but also from the need to prevent incursions from neighboring provinces during times of dispute. The Gupta and Mogul dynasties, for example, jealously guarded their wealth and territory with state-of-the-art fortifications.

Sometimes these forts had as much an ornamental purpose as a military one. The Red Fort, for example, seems to exude an air of martial muscle as well as artistic refinement. It seems to say to an onlooker (or invader), "Do you dare to try and capture and destroy something so beautiful?"

Octagonal in shape, like most Islamic forts in India, it is not strategically well-placed, but is very intimidating nonetheless. Amazingly, it was built (for the Emperor Shah Jahan) in only nine years. Its beautifully proportioned lines and rich sandstone walls—which, in the rays of the rising or setting sun, give the place its name—are regarded as being among the summits of Mogul culture.

Far Left: The beautiful ruddy façade of the Amber Fort in Agra, India.
Left: The rich interior of one of India's many palaces.

The immaculate detail of this white stone building is a typical feature of the traditional Indian palaces and forts.

Forts and Palaces

Above: The Fort Watchtower in Rajasthan.
Right: Vibrant colors are a typical feature of traditional Indian architecture.

Another example of a fort that combines strong defense with ornament is Gwalior Fort. Originally built in the 8th century, it was described by the Mogul emperor Babur as "the pearl in the necklace of the castles of Hind [India]." Yet it had seen bitter fighting between the Tomara and Scindhia dynasties, among others. Each conqueror repaired the damage and sought to make the structure even more pleasing to the eye. Once again, function (as a fort) and form (as an object of beauty) have been melded perfectly.

The place to go for this hybrid building style is the Rajasthani city of Jaipur, the Pink City of India. It is hard to know where to start in this metropolis—dusty, crazy, and thronged with people, *tuk-tuks*, and bicycles. But these intrusions of modern life immediately vanish from the mind with just one glance at the modest, but perfectly-formed, Nahargarh Fort. Built by the city's founder, Jai Singh, in 1734—seven years after he brought Jaipur into being—it is once again an expert amalgam of Hindu and Muslim styles, although on a surprisingly small, neat scale.

Its elevated position and threatening cannons seem to suggest the fort had a primarily military function, but, in reality, it never fired a shot, nor was it ever fired on. In 1880, the Maharajah Sawai Madho Singh converted the fort into a pleasure palace of great opulence and a retreat from the summer monsoon season.

The Amber Fort, a few miles away, looms out of the hillside as though part of the living rock itself. This is where the Rajputs, who founded Jaipur state, had their capital from the 11th century until Jai Singh founded Jaipur city.

The Amber Fort (pronounced Amer) is a particular favorite with tourists because of the elephant ride from the valley floor up the winding, walled road to the fort's great entrance. As the region's seat of government, the focus

was on immense fortifications rather than particularly fancy ornamentation. This at least applies to the exterior. Inside, the Amber Fort's serenity and the beauty of its carvings, moldings, and sculptures as beautiful as anything found on the subcontinent.

The same goes for the huge and forbidding Golconda Fort with its four, square granite terraces sitting 120 feet (36.5 m) high on a hill near Hyderabad in the Deccan plateau. Again, this was the home of the local rulers, the Qutub Shahi kings, around 600 years ago and a natural target for aggressors. Nonetheless, behind this massive and unforgiving exterior—the gates are fitted with enormous, vicious-looking spikes to prevent elephant-mounted troops from attacking and breaking in—lie gorgeous water gardens and smaller palaces. These were intended for the leisure of the emperor's family and retinue, and much of what remains clearly follows Islamic design patterns.

Back in Rajasthan, perhaps the most perfect coupling of aesthetics and strategy is the amazing Jaisalmer Fort. Located not far from Jaipur, in the desolate midst of the Thar Desert (which literally means "the home of the dead"), its vivid golden mass rises as if from nowhere, like a mirage. When struck by the sun, it appears encrusted with gold. In the moonlight, it is hauntingly lilac in color, and, in the stillness of the desert, it seems strangely out of place. For all its stupendous beauty and delicacy of stonework and carving, and the purity of architectural line and proportion, it was built with a defensive plan in mind.

It was the work of a local ruler, Raja Jaisal, in 1156. His nearby capital, Lodurva, was too vulnerable to invasion and plunder, he decreed, and so he built this fantastic structure and the settlement around it. Its hilltop location certainly implies that military concerns were first in Raja Jaisal's mind, but creating a masterpiece in stone must have been an issue for him too.

Modern Architecture in India

The roots of Indian modern architecture lie in the British withdrawal and the end of colonial rule in 1947. The partition of India and the civil war that followed meant that Indian authorities had other things to worry about than commissioning architects to maintain India's ancient building traditions.

In the colonial era, the British architect Sir Edwin Lutyens (1867-1944) had built some fine buildings in Indian cities for the benefit of the colonial administration. These were hardly examples of cutting-edge modernism, but they combined grandeur with an austere and minimal elegance. What were Indian architects to do? Were they to continue Sir Edwin's work or celebrate their Indian identity of the pre-Colonial past? Were they to be influenced by Hindu or Muslim or Buddhist styles? Or were they to embrace the styles of Western Europe?

The issue began to resolve itself in the 1950s when two schools of thought arose: a Revivalist faction and a Modernist faction. Neither got far. Revivalism failed in constructing styles that emphasized continuity with the past. Modernists were too quick to impose a conventional European imprint on India's cities, because it looked out of place. But, in 1956, Jawaharlal Nehru, India's first prime minister, organized a competition to design the Ashoka Hotel in Delhi. B.E. Doctor, the Bombay architect, won with an ingenious, seemingly pillarless space inspired by Islamic, Hindu, British, and modern styles.

The European modernist architect Le Corbusier was commissioned to design the entire town of Chandigarh, which he did on a three-part plan, viewed as a human body. The "head" was to contain official buildings, the "body" a complex of educational and residential buildings, and the "feet" the industrial part of town. Le Corbusier also designed the town's High Court and Assembly buildings.

Le Corbusier and Doctor's striking achievements seemed to revitalize young Indian architects. Probably the most-photographed modern building in India is Sabha's Bahai Temple in Delhi. Blending the forms of India's past, it is a vast, stunning swan-white structure—a huge and elegant creation that communicates both majesty and great serenity. Other notable architecture includes Raj Rewal's work in designing business, sporting, and residential facilities for the athletes and officials of the 1982 Asian Games in New Delhi.

The lack of money—and the channeling of any available funds into strengthening the economy and infrastructure—starve many of India's architects of resources. It still remains to be seen if the World Centre of Vedic Learning in Jabalpur, Madhya Pradesh, will be built. At 2,222 feet (677 m) high, this would be the world's tallest building and will be modeled on Sao Paulo's Brazil Tower. With younger architects such as Charles Correa, Prashant Diwakriti, and Vineet Chadha still honing their skills, there could be exciting times ahead for Indian architecture.

Right: The India Arch in Delhi is an example of the European influence on Indian architecture.
Far Right: The modern and fluid Lotus Temple in New Delhi.

The grand Palace of Tipu illuminated at night.

Diversity

Music

The hum of the multi-stringed *sitar* is the most recognizable sound of Indian music. But these beautiful instruments are only the tiniest corner of a universe of sublime artistic talent. Like so many other aspects of India, there is a new experience for the traveler in practically every town and village. It has links to religion, dance, and art.

If it is possible to generalize about Indian music, it is possible to divide it into the traditions of the north (Hindustani) and the south (Karnatic), although this applies largely only to classical music of the former royal courts. Persian music influenced the north in the 15th century with religious *dhrupavad* music developing into a form of singing called *dhrupad*. This is "the rendering of verse into song." Another, more complex form, is the more romantic and expressive *Khayal*, which developed three centuries later. Each style evolved in connection with local folk music as it spread throughout India. The northern *Khayal* is based more on singing, and follows a scale that is recognizable to western ears.

Southern Indian (Karnatic) music is based even more on the use of the human voice, with most compositions having many parts sung in varying order. Most renowned of these is the *kiriti*, a sophisticated song form.

Raga (melody) and *tala* (rhythm) are central to both styles of music, and they have enabled both styles to blend with local folk and religious elements. *Raga* is almost unbelievably complex, designed to provoke both the heart and the mind. There are separate *ragas* for any time during a 24-hour day depending on the listener's mood.

To Western ears, a fine *tala* is often amazing, because of the complexity of the rhythms.

The numerous faiths in India mean that devotional music is still alive and well, and that it is often of awesome finesse and depth. The Sikhs have their *shabads*, or mystical songs, sung by the wandering 10th century holy man Guru Nanak. He traveled all over India using these ancient melodies to spread Sikhism's message of love. East Bengali boatmen sing the emotionally charged *bhatiyali* to their gods whilst on the waters. The *qawwali* style has become well-known in the West thanks to the efforts of virtuoso vocalists like the late Nusrat Fateh Ali Khan. Astonishing singers like him evolved out of the Muslim Sufi sect around the 10th century, and its intense songs were first heard in India around the 12th century.

Almost as diverse as Indian music is the vast range of beautiful musical instruments—wind, percussion, string—that have developed over the centuries. These also illustrate how much the main styles of Indian classical music have been shaped by folk music instruments.

There is a great wealth of string instruments: the mighty sitar and other plucked instruments, which are used as "drones," bowed violin-like devices (*Dilruba* in the north, *Esraj* in the south), and the hammered dulcimer-like *santoor*.

Drums—the *tabla*, or double drum, and the common man's drum, the little cylinder-shaped *dholak*—are usually played with the hands; but the ornate and large-scale *nagara*, with its steel shell, is played with sticks. Some of these have been so large that they have been nearly impossible to play. Instead, they are used as monuments to mark the entrance to cities and towns.

While many Western music styles and instruments are now important to the production of modern Indian music, it is still possible to trace 15 centuries of varied musical history through the Indipop and Bollywood soundtracks heard on every radio in India today—from bars in Bombay to the tiniest Himalayan village.

Left: The *tambura*, one of India's classical string instruments.

Far Left: The multi-stringed *sitar* is the most recognizable sound within traditional Indian music.

Dance

Classical forms

Indian classical dance, as with so much of the subcontinent's cultural life, is linked to religious ritual. The six best-known forms of classical dance are all related to the worshipping of gods through the re-telling of myths and legends. As with music, there are folk forms in India, usually reserved for family or local festivals, but these have become intertwined with classical forms.

There are three fundamentals in Indian dance—*natya*, the interpretation of a character through dance, *nritta*, dance as technique, and *nritya*, expression of mood through dance movements. Indian dance is less dependent on the movement of the legs than most Western classical dance. Instead, a great variety of head movements (at least 13), eye movements (36), and hand movements (67) offer the Indian dancer a vast emotional range to play with. Movement of the torso and the spine, and the rhythmic use of the feet (many Indian dancers have bells around their ankles) add to the rhythmic frenzy of the music. Most recognizable to Westerners as a "traditional" dance is probably the graceful and flowing *bharatya natya*. Usually performed by women, it is characterized by the adopted stance: the feet flat on the floor save for rhythmic lifts of the heel, and subtle movements of the torso and upper body. The arms are all-important, and strong elbows are needed for support. The 67 *mudras*, or hand movements, are incredibly complicated and can convey different meanings if the palm of the hand is cupped or spread out.

Bharatya natya is not alone, however; there are other respected forms of classical dance in the subcontinent. One, the *manipuri*, comes from the remote northeastern frontier state of Manipur. It is defined by ornate, but stylized, circular motions and is said to mirror the movement of the planets around the sun. It is again rooted in Hindu mythology and a dance performed by Lords Radha and Krishna. It finds expression today in the famous *Ras Lila* dance of the region.

Kathak, a nimble and rhythmically complex dance from the northern state of Uttar Pradesh, again reflects the exploits of Radha and Krishna. The arrival of the Moguls altered its form slightly in the 17th century, when the Muslim rulers adopted it as a form of entertainment. It lost some of its expressive and emotional depth and became more of a technical exercise.

Far Left: A sculpture depicting the Indian Lord of the Dance.

Left: Traditional Indian dance involves intricate clothing, makeup, and jewelry.

Dance

Orissa state has the *Odissi*, a sensuous, almost erotic dance of devotion to Lord Krishna, utilizing the bust, torso, and head. *Odissi* dancers can be seen in gorgeous sculptures on temple walls at Bhubaneshwar, Puri, and Konark.

The performers of *Kuchipudi*, from Andhra Pradesh, sing as well as dance. This, rather like *Kathakali*, is more drama than pure dance.

While the classical, or court, repertoire dominates the world's view of Indian dances, there are still individual local traditions that remain. Some of these are extremely exotic, like the grotesquely masked sword dancing of the *Brita* (or *Vrita*) of West Bengal. There is even a dance on stilts,

performed by the children of the Gond tribe of Madhya Pradesh. These little dancers are so skilled that they can perform elaborate steps on their stilts—even in water and on marshy ground—and often finish their performances in a precarious pyramid formation.

India's dances have always appealed far beyond its frontiers. Ethnologists believe that the movements and gestures used in Japanese fan dancing, for example, owe much to Indian influences. The same can be said of the formalized temple dancers of Java. With such an effortless accumulation of grace and technique over so many centuries, this preeminence is hardly surprising.

Far Right: An Indian dancer demonstrating the art of the traditional *bharatya natya* dance.

Right: The colorful dresses, or saris, of eastern India are an important dance feature.

Below: Rajasthan dress.

Pottery

As befits a country as vast and diverse as India, its pottery is famed for its variety of styles, glazes, and forms.

If we survey the regions of India from north to south, we begin with Kashmir and earthenware of ordinary clay, but with a curious glaze. The district of Kangra, in Himachal Pradesh, is rightly famous for its clayware.

Delhi's blue pottery is perhaps India's best-known example of the craft. Persian blue is the name given to the dye that gives the clay its distinctive color. A glaze and a high-temperature firing in the kiln makes Delhi pottery stand out even more. It also makes it tough and durable, something valued by some Indian consumers who might not be able to replace a broken pot or mug easily.

West Bengal boasts the curious Mansa pottery, representing the forbidding snake goddess. Usually this takes the form of a curved pot with a grotesque hand-painted face. Bengal's pottery traditions have also produced the strange *Dakshinirai* pots. These are crowned with a sharp edge, which signifies a god who protects man against the marauding tiger.

The luster of Uttar Pradesh's elaborate *Chunar* pottery comes from a powder called *kabiz*, a secret formula derived from the mud of rice fields. Famous for its black clay pottery, Uttar Pradesh produces some of the finest and most decorative *Chunar*, which is inlaid with silver paint in intricate designs. The art was perfected in Nizamabad, but the province also produces the inexpensive, tough tableware from Khurja.

Western Rajasthan produces narrow-necked pots (a good idea in a desert region) with gorgeous relief sculptures of gods and goddesses. In Gujarat, white and black clay artifacts are sun-dried before being carefully painted. Jaipur earthenware is made from Egyptian paste, a self-glazing substance, and is fragile and decorative. In the south, there are a number of places renowned for their pottery, such as Goa, Vellore, and Arcot in the State of Tamil Nadu. The latter's *chilums*, or clay pipes, are famed for their refinement, as are the examples of preservation jars.

Pondicherry, in the deep south of India, meanwhile, is probably the most renowned centre of pottery in the whole of the subcontinent. Delicate china clay is the tool of choice here, and the results, beautifully crafted and matured at high temperatures, are breathtaking.

Once again, every region has its own style, its own way of doing things. The "clay-glazing" or the strange orange-peel textures of some of the works by Pondicherry craftsmen are good examples of this.

Bottom Left: Earthenware pottery before it undergoes the glazing process.
Center: One of many designs found on Indian earthenware.
Right: The art of pottery exists throughout India, with varying styles, colors, and shapes.

The snake goddess typical to the unique style of Mansa pottery.

Jewelry

Jewelry has always been important in India. Ancient texts report that people fashioned jewelry out of seeds, feathers, animal teeth and bones, berries, fruits, and flowers. The famous Mohenjodaro archaeological digs of the 20th century brought many beautiful items of the Indus Valley civilization to the world's attention. Men and women alike delighted in adorning themselves with gold, copper, silver, ivory, and bronze, not to mention precious stones.

This is perhaps to be expected. After all, the sacred texts of the Ramayana and the Mahabharata describe bodily adornment, and the code of Manu defines the duties of the goldsmith. India's rich resources of precious stones have undoubtedly encouraged this trend.

To each region its own style. Jaipur has its Mogul-influenced, exquisite enameling, known as metacarpi, which is often used for chokers and necklaces. Delhi is renowned for its settings of precious stones in gold. Silver seems particularly present in India, from Rajasthan and Gujarat to Madhya Pradesh. There is also the filigree work, using very fine strands of silver, common to Orissa and Andhra Pradesh. The intricacy of the silversmiths' work in Himachal Pradesh is a true wonder.

Gold and silverware, in the form of earrings or necklaces, are inspired by the traditions of eastern Assam and southern Tamil Nadu. The orchid and the lokaparo, a motif of two birds back to back, are Assamese specialties. The jewelry of Nagaland incorporates shells, animal claws, and other natural elements. The cobra's hood is a more sinister and sensual motif in Tamil Nadu.

In the far north, in the remote mountain hideaway of Ladakh, locals create the most gorgeous headdresses, featuring cornelian, turquoise, and agate. The earth provides the jewels, and, in a country as vast as India, the artisans have invented a multitude of ways to set them. And most are very beautiful indeed.

Far Left: Beaded and embroidered items are typically used at Indian wedding ceremonies.
Left: Silverwork, like this teapot that incorporates stones and carvings, is typical of the crafts found throughout the country.
Right: Colorful bangles.

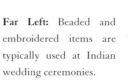

The Tibetan-influenced jewelry of the northern town of Ladakh is made with turquoise, carnelian, and agate.

These traditional Indian puppets are just one of many crafts found throughout India.

Diversity

Food

The one thing that Westerners often misunderstand about India is food. For a start, there is no such thing as an Indian meal, since one can choose from so many styles, and many Westerners will rarely have the same eating habits as Indians.

Indians have their main meal at lunchtime. Often they will eat with their hands, but there is a certain etiquette. For instance, the hands must never touch the mouth. Pre-packed meals are designed to be eaten with the hands, although using a knife and fork is never frowned upon. Throughout India, vegetarian cuisine is favored, as are wheaten flatbreads.

This, of course, depends on regional variations, and there are so many. Punjabis gave the world

the *tandoor*, the hot clay oven used to cook tandoori meals, which is heated to high temperatures over coal fires. The great and cultured Moguls, from the 16th century onwards, helped introduce the sweetening and refining influence of yogurt and dairy products into Punjabi dishes, which make them some of India's most delicious.

Gujarat's *thalis*—one-plate feasts including a lentil-based *dhal*—are gaining popularity in the West. In Maharashtra, people consume meat and fish in abundance, enhanced by the sweet and powerful taste of peanuts and cashews.

The further south one travels, the hotter the spices tend to be. In the southern states of Kerala and Karnataka, the food is mainly

vegetarian, and often served on a giant banana leaf. Here, though, the coconut is a staple and used as a sweet contrast to the hot and sour spices. Another southern staple is rice. It forms the basis of the *idli*, a battered and steamed rice cake, which is often eaten with a lethally hot mix of spices, vegetables, pepper, and pulses called *sambar*.

The coasts of India, of course, encourage people to eat fish and seafood, in all kinds of wonderfully intoxicating local recipes. Bengal is particularly famed for its fish and for the mix of spices in which it is cooked—a combination of "pachphoron" (or aniseed), cumin seed, black cumin seed, mustard, and fenugreek.

Left: Some of the colorful chilies that fill spicy southern Indian cuisine.

Bottom Right: Delicious triangle *samosas*.

A sampling of the vibrant dishes that can be found all over this gastronomic country.

Spices

Some say that spices were grown in India before 3000 BC. This is unconfirmed, but what evidence there is suggests these spices— such as turmeric, black pepper, and mustard—were from the northern regions.

In Biblical times, writers told of the great variety and glories of what they considered "Arab" spices. In fact, most Arab spices had come from India, or were bought from Chinese and Javanese merchants resident in Indian ports. Frankincense and myrrh, brought to Bethlehem by the Three Kings for the infant Christ, were expensive and sensual gifts from "the East"—could this have meant from India? Those great patrons of specialist cuisine, the 16th and 17th century Mogul emperors, enjoyed a highly-flavored style of cooking, full of color and deeply exotic tastes. This was when Indian spices became a big business. Around the same period, the first traders from the West— sailing from Portugal, Spain, Britain, and the Netherlands to the Indian Ocean— found the sensual, stimulating tastes and hues of India's spices irresistible. The coast of Kerala around the port of Cochin (now Kochi), which is dominated by the spice-filled tropical forests, became known as the Spice Coast.

From the Ghats mountain range, in the middle of the subcontinent, merchants would float boatloads of ginger, cardamom, and cinnamon down rivers and through wetland canals to the ports of Madras (Chennai), Cochin (Kochi), and Calicut (Kozhikode). Pepper was particularly prized by the Europeans of the Renaissance, just as it had been by the Roman Empire. Chinese and other Far Eastern merchants also came in search of the spices of India—not just for the flavors, but also for the scents, which even today are used as natural air fresheners all over India. They range from the delicate to the powerful, but all are sensory pleasures.

Over the years, with the evolution of Indian cuisine in the subcontinent's individual states, different spices have come to the fore. Uttar Pradesh is probably India's most prolific region in terms of the range of spices grown: chili (most varieties were actually imported from the New World via European merchants), aniseed, coriander, fennel, cumin, fenugreek, mustard, and turmeric. Tamil Nadu, part of the Spice Coast of centuries ago, still produces the cinnamon for which it is famed, as well as cloves, herbal and unnamed local "exotic spices", and rare varieties like pomegranate seeds. The obscure state of Sikkim in the Himalayas produces *Tejpat*, a type of olive-green cassia leaf. Another Himalayan state, Kashmir, specializes in *Kokam*, a round, purple fruit. *Garam Masala*, a mixture of spices, has found favor in the West.

India's spice production now totals 3.2 billion tons a year, and is now one of Indian agriculture's most important sectors. But at its core, much of the spice trading in India is still a cheerfully down-to-earth industry. Spices are harvested, placed in sacks, and sped in ancient trucks along rough roads to markets and warehouses in towns and cities. Some cinnamon and nutmeg still comes to town in the boats of poor farmers the way it did 500 years ago.

In Kerala, some of the finest spices on the subcontinent are sorted in almost derelict spice warehouses. Stray dogs wander around, and the noise of motor-rickshaws, or *tuk-tuks*, roars outside in puddle-filled streets; but the air is full of the most wonderful perfumes— sun-dried ginger, cloves, and nutmeg. Indian street markets—from the high plateaus of the Karakoram to the steaming tropics of Tamil Nadu—are vivid with color as cardamoms and chilies glow in the sunshine.

It is as exciting, refined, and satisfying an experience as the balance of flavors in a good Indian meal.

Below: A typical jug used for carrying and storing water— an important antidote to spice!

Right: Cinnamon is an important spice in Indian cooking and can be found in traditional tea.

The southern states of Kerala and Karnataka use a variety of vegetables in their regional cuisine.

Tea

India is the largest exporter of tea in the world. Tea is grown mainly on plantations in the foothills of the Himalayas in northeastern India, where the rainy climate and hilly terrain are suitable for the tea bushes. The regions of Assam and Darjeeling have lent their names to varieties of black tea that are enjoyed all over the world.

Tea leaves grow on bushy plants that can grow up to 8–10 feet tall (2.5–3 m) or more, but are usually trimmed to waist height when they are cultivated. The leaves are picked by hand. The choicest parts of the tea plant are the young buds on the tips of branches and the first two or three leaves. Tea leaves that are harvested early in the year, after the spring rains, have a more delicate flavor than those picked in the summer months. After the tea leaves are picked, they are dried in environments carefully controlled for temperature and humidity. The leaves also start to oxidize, which causes changes to their color and chemical composition, and therefore the flavor of the beverages they produce. Green tea is made from leaves that have been dried for only a short time, while leaves for black tea are dried longer and therefore undergo more oxidation. This gives black tea a stronger flavor than green tea. Both types of tea come from the same plant species, though: *Camellia sinensis*.

Right and Below: The tea of India is world famous and remains one of the central features of Indian culinary delights.

Himalayas

Without question the mightiest mountain range in the world—rivaled only by its near neighbor the Karakoram—the Himalayas dominate India's northern frontiers from Jammu and Kashmir in the west to the northeastern frontier states. Characterized by soaring mountains—many peaks are higher than 26,000 feet (8,000 m)—and graceful snow-capped peaks, and the Himalayas also boast massive river gorges. Among these passages, rocky and forested by turns, is the mighty Brahmaputra canyon.

The mountains also act as a climatic barrier. They mark the transition from the humid, subtropical weather systems of India's plains and hills to the dry, arid desert climates of central Asia. They help contain India's weather and are instrumental in making it what it is. For instance, the northbound monsoon rains are forced to lose most of their moisture on the Indian side of the range, thereby leaving the northern, Tibetan side relatively dry. The Himalayas themselves, despite their peaks being blanketed in eternal snow, have a temperate

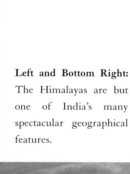

Left and Bottom Right:
The Himalayas are but one of India's many spectacular geographical features.

Alpine climate and a lot of lush vegetation. The geography of the region, though, makes farming difficult, if not impossible. As a result, the predominantly Buddhist inhabitants of these thinly populated regions concentrate largely on herding animals, although some arable farming exists on fertile, grassland plateaus.

There are also the tranquil lakes of Kashmir, which—until recent local unrest—were such a haven for tourists. The same was true back in the days of the British rule, or *Raj*, when it was a blessing to come to such a serene and cool place, far from the teeming heat of the subcontinental plain.

The ethereal peaks, which seem to reach high into the heavens, are said to be inhabited by ghosts and spirits; animism, or the belief in spirits, is still widespread in the remotest parts of Himalayan India. Although not located in India, Mount Everest, the world's highest peak, was first measured by Sir George Everest's great expedition to map the whole of the subcontinent.

Himalayas

Ladakh

This is a real jewel, secret and reclusive, in one of India's remotest corners—a tiny piece of Himalayan paradise only recently discovered by Western visitors. Were it not for ongoing civil disturbances in Kashmir, of which it is a part, it would surely be even more popular. As it is, difficult transport links mean that it is relatively unspoiled.

Its 45,174 square miles (117,000 sq km) nestle in the lap of the Himalayan Ladakh Range, where the peaks of the snowy mountains reach far above 26,000 feet (8000 m). There are high grassy plains where sheep and cattle graze, and great river canyons. The region is part of the upper Indus Valley, where one of India's great waterways has its source high among the glaciers. The Ladakh plain slopes gently upwards from the West, where the barren moonscape of Rupshu Zaskar lies. Here, temperatures can fall low enough to keep even hardy cattle farmers, and their animals, indoors for much of the year, They might venture out only to forage for *tamarisk* (a shrub) or *furze* (a grass) to burn as fuel for their fires. Other Ladakhis concentrate on farming the more fertile valleys around the regional capital Leh, which lies about 125 miles (200 km) east of the Pakistani border. Pakistan and India have a long-standing dispute about the status and "ownership" of the whole state of Jammu and Kashmir, including Ladakh.

It all seems a long way from this placid and unspoiled portion of a world that time forgot, where ancient Buddhist practices—and animist spirit beliefs—flourish as in few other locations on the Indian subcontinent.

Bottom Left: Tibetan prayer flags atop a local mountain in Ladakh.
Center: Just one of the pristine river canyons of this Himalayan region.
Right: The blue sky of Ladakh radiates against the white clouds.

One of the many Buddhist rock formations found in the regions surrounding the majestic Himalayas.

A classical Indian Buddhist *stupa* surrounded by deep snow in the foothills of Mount Everest.

The Plains

Agriculture

Left: One of India's many agricultural regions.
Below: Small farmers still make up the majority of India's farming.
Bottom Right: Various grains, such as lentils and maize, are grown in India.

It is a familiar sight to Westerners—the lone farmer driving an oxcart, or plowing a sodden field behind a bullock and a rusty harrow in the shimmering late-afternoon heat. The conclusions are often all too easy to draw. Indian farming means subsistence, poverty, crops washed away by unforgiving monsoons or floods—it means hunger.

Yet the reality can be, and often is, different. Things in India are certainly changing, and, in any case, Indian agriculture has not always meant a hand-to-mouth existence.

First, some facts and figures. The Great Plains of the North are also known as the Indo-Gangetic Plain, which encompasses three great rivers: the Indus, Ganges, and Brahmaputra. It covers a vast area, including the states of Assam, Punjab, Haryana, West Bengal, the Union Territory of Chandigarh, and a corner of Bihar. It is one of the world's largest flood plains and, for a rural area, it is very densely populated, with 1180 people per square mile (456 people per sq km). The majority of those who live in the country are farmers. This "breadbasket of India" was once so rich that it became home to emperors of the Maurya and Gupta dynasties.

The land is more fertile than most might think, owing to the large amounts of silt deposited by a complex system of rivers. Despite the area being quite well-irrigated, the farmers welcome a good monsoon season to water their crops of rice and wheat.

Sugarcane, maize (Indian corn), and cotton are also key crops on the plains. Small farmers do much of the cultivating, although larger farming businesses are increasingly buying up small plots.

In the 1960s, high-yield seeds were planted in the plains to increase production—since India's population was growing faster than its agricultural sector could sustain. The backbreaking labor may be a thing of the past one day, because India's agriculture, still facing a population explosion, is once again responding to demand.

Flooding is still a problem against which agriculture must be permanently vigilant—especially when the Ganges, Indus, or Brahmaputra swell with melting snow from the Himalayas, or from heavy monsoon rains.

Bodies of Water

Lakes, Rivers, and Oceans

India's coastline is 4720 miles (7600 km) long. From Kolkata Port in the east, it runs southwest through such historic ports as Chennai and Cochin, famous for their role in opening up sea routes to India and in the country's eventual colonization. Passing Goa, it then heads north again through Mumbai, to Kandla, Gujarat state's main outlet of goods to the Arabian Sea. There are many, mostly small, islands along the way; the most famous and scenically most beautiful being Goa, with its emerald palm trees, creamy-white sands, and turquoise ocean.

India has always had a close relationship with the sea—not so much as a seafaring nation, but as a trading one. The coastline is densely populated and fishing is a livelihood for many.

Goa's attractions have made it a tourist mecca in the last few decades, and whereas India's coastline has yet to achieve a high-profile tourist industry, its inland lakes are quickly growing in popularity with foreign travelers. These include the beautiful hill lakes of Rajasthan. This area, most of which is desert, also has cool uplands and the gorgeous city of Udaipur. Built on the edges of three lakes, including the tranquil Lake Pichola, it is renowned as "the Venice of the East." Other lakes in the region include Pushkar Lake—considered sacred by Hindus—which lies on the edge of the desert to the north of Udaipur.

The North, with its Himalayan foothills, boasts lakes like the gigantic Bhimtal. Set in a lovely but neglected part of India known as Uttarakhand, the lake is rapidly becoming a valuable source of tourist income.

Not all lakes are natural features; as early as the 18th century, in Uttar Pradesh, the local ruler, Raja Parikshit, ordered the digging of the Belasagar, a huge reservoir, which serves to irrigate farmland in the area.

In the southeast, in Kerala state, where fishing is a way of life and houseboats of every shape and size provide homes for many people, lies the large, fertile Ashtamudi Lake with its strange marshy inlets. Another well-known body of water is Chilika Lake, which is situated on the eastern coast in Orissa, and is a blend of salt marsh and fresh water.

The wetlands around these areas are characteristic of many low-lying lakes in the country. However, the most famous wetlands are associated with India's great rivers—the Indus, the Ganges, and the Brahmaputra—which flow over thousands of miles down from the Himalaya and Karakoram mountain ranges.

The Indus and Ganges dominate the northern plains and, despite having brought disastrous floods over the centuries, they have provided generations of farmers with essential irrigation. To the Hindus both rivers are sacred, and, on feast days, pilgrims can be seen flocking in their millions to bathe in the holy waters from *ghats*, or ceremonial flights of stone steps.

Right: India is host to many beautiful beaches.

Far Right: Lakes are most common in the northern regions surrounding the Himalayas.

Diversity

Religion

As befits a country of so many millions of people, India has an astonishing array of religious beliefs. The principal ones are Hinduism, Jainism, Sikhism, Islam, Christianity, Zoroastrianism, Judaism, and Baha'i. There are other minor faiths in remote corners of the subcontinent, and the leading religions also host innumerable subsects.

Hindu faith traces its roots in the subcontinent back to 300 BC, and Hindus now make up the vast majority of the Indian population. However, Buddhism and Jainism also played an early part in the development of the country, as we know it today.

Buddhism was the state religion of India from the 3rd century BC. Jainism was the creation of Mahavira, otherwise known as "the great hero," whose fundamental Hinduism was moderated by his rejection of the caste system and the belief in the cycle of births.

Religious tolerance was crucial to India's development for centuries. The great Buddhist ruler Asoka respected Hindu beliefs, which encouraged the rise of Hinduism around a thousand years ago.

By this time, a new religion had appeared in India: Islam. Missionaries of the new faith appeared in India in the 7th century, and by the 11th and 12th centuries, the decline of Buddhism was allowing Islamic incomers to convert many people in the northwest of India—now Pakistan—and also in the Indian states of Gujarat and Rajasthan. The all-conquering Moguls of the 15th and 16th centuries may have raided and subdued much of north India, but mostly they were wise and benign rulers, who encouraged religions to coexist peacefully.

Jainism was sidelined in favor of the larger faiths, although today there are still some three million Jains practicing in India. Buddhism, meanwhile, survives at the extreme ends of India—in the mountainous north and in some isolated areas of the southern tip of the subcontinent. It is much more widespread on the island of Sri Lanka.

The mysterious Zoroastrians have always been a minority. Originating in 2600 BC, with the rediscovery of the teachings of the prophet Zoroaster, or Zarathustra (ca. 6000 BC), their faith revolves around fire-worship. Fire, for Zoroastrians, represents truth and righteousness, the force of good that Ahura Mazda, the one true god, embodied in his eternal struggle against the forces of evil.

Today's Zoroastrians, or Parsis, have substantially different social outlooks thanks to the efforts, in the 1850s, of the Rehnumai Mazdayasan Sabha (Religious Reform Association), which sought to destroy orthodoxy and improve the status of women. Of India's current 90,000 Parsis, the majority live in the west, in Maharashtra and Gujarat states.

Sikhism is the second most recent of India's great faiths. Less than 650 years old, it is now the world's fifth-largest religion in terms of numbers of adherents. It was only in 1500 that Guru Nanak, the founder of Sikhism, broke away from Hinduism and Islam. Sikhism is another religion with a single god—not humanly present, but spiritually represented by ten *gurus*, or followers.

In 1599, Guru Gobind Singh reorganized the Sikh religion along more formal lines (it was then that the distinctive turban, beard, and other aspects of Sikh culture first appeared). It was also to be a military force, charged with defending the faith.

Hinduism's resurgence in India came with the arrival—in large numbers—of Christians in the 18th and 19th centuries.

Of course, Christians had visited the subcontinent before. St. Thomas is said to have landed there as a missionary in 52 AD. Much later, Christian missionaries accompanied merchants and traders to India and attempted conversions. They had little success, except in tiny enclaves along the coasts. But the colonization of India in the 1700s and 1800s changed that, and there are

now some 30 million Christian Indians, or 2.3 percent of the population. Interestingly, these Christian communities are still largely rooted where the more recent Christian missionaries first arrived—in the south and around Kolkata and Bengal.

India's Jews, though, are scattered throughout the country. They form four groups: the Children of Israel set down roots in Mararashtra; the *Cochinis* in Kerala (the capital of which, Cochin, has a quarter named Jewtown); the *Baghdadis*, descended from Persian, Iraqi, and Syrian Jewish traders in Mumbai, Pune and Calcutta; and the obscure Manipuri Jews. Living in the secluded state of Manipur, on the Indian-Myanmar border, they believe themselves to be descendants of a Jewish community that escaped Assyrian persecution in Biblical times. The Cochin Jews were the most successful of these dispersed communities. They prospered economically, and the Keralan emperor Bhaskara Ravi Varman granted them privileges and freedoms as early as 1000 AD. The world-famous

Below: The serene face of the Buddha can be found all over the country.

Right: Meditation is a key feature of Buddhism, one of India's major religions.

Jewish Copper Plate was given to the emperor by as a sign of gratitude from the community. The Christian Portuguese attempted to reverse their freedoms in 1565, but the British and Dutch later restored the Jews' privileges.

The Baha'i House in Delhi, one of the most striking examples of modern Indian architecture, is the most public representation of the egalitarian Baha'i faith. Brought to India from Iran in 1863, it now boasts 2.2 million followers in the subcontinent.

Animism, or the belief in holy spirits incarnated in nature, exists in some northern tribal areas—principally in the wild northeast, where India meets Tibet and Myanmar. There are, however, many other beliefs specific to different towns and villages. This is confirmed by the vast variations in the architecture of India's innumerable places of worship.

Whatever the religion, India remains a profoundly spiritual place, and one in which most communities still respect the spirituality of others.

Gods and Deities

Hinduism

Left: Lord Ganesh, the part-human, part-elephant deity, is the Remover of Obstacles in Hinduism.
Below: Blue-bodied Shiva is often depicted as the Lord of the Dance.

Of all the world's great religions, Hinduism must have the most complex mythology. To explain it would require a very long book, a good storyteller, and a patient listener. In one famous example, it was claimed—probably with only slight exaggeration—that there are some 330 million deities on the subcontinent.

Yet to learn of their exploits and their place in Hinduism is to take a captivating trip into the imagination and the soul. Anyone who is introduced to Hinduism's great array of gods, goddesses, and demons will always want to know more.

The *Rig Veda*, the oldest existing Hindu scripture, speaks of the divine's embodiment in Saguna Brahman, less of a god than a set of eternal truths. Hindus worship Saguna Brahman in the form of gods, who were, or are, more or less real. These include the mother goddesses like Kali and Durga, but there are countless other deities worshipped by the Hindus. They appear everywhere—on charm bracelets, garlanded with flowers in garden shrines, dangling from the rear-view mirrors of *tuk-tuks*. But why?

Hindus believe that God exists but is unknowable except through the deities Lord Vishnu, Lord Brahma, and Lord Shiva, who were called upon to perform the cosmic tasks of creation, preservation, dissolution, and recreation. This trinity (or *trimurti*) is not separate, merely three incarnations of one Supreme Being.

The deities' works are charted in the sacred scriptures of Hinduism: the *Rig Veda*, the *Samaveda*, the *Bhagavad Gita*, and *Atharva Veda*. These contain numerous subsidiary scriptures, including, for example, the Agamas, which describe how to worship gods and deities.

To non-Hindus, the best-known deity is Lord Vishnu. Second in the *trimurti*, he is responsible for the protection of the universe and will come to the aid of the world when it is threatened by great evil. Some Hindus worship only Vishnu, regarding the other two members of the *trimurti* as inferior, or demigods.

Vishnu is associated largely with the Sun, of light and life. He has been incarnated in Rama, the fierce man, and in Krishna, greatest of warriors and hero of the Indian epic drama the *Mahabharata*. There have been eight other forms, including Narasimha the Lion and Buddha, the wise man. We will read more about them later.

Vishnu is usually depicted in human form, riding on the back of Garuda the Eagle. Bearing a beatific smile and with bluish skin, he carries a number of items in his four hands: a conch shell, with which to utter the holy word "Om"; the *chakra*, or discus, a symbol of the mind; the mace, or scepter, of physical power; and the lotus flower, symbol of joy and liberation. His consort is Lakshmi, the dazzling goddess of wealth, knowledge, and purity. She is also the goddess of hard work, which means that many Hindus have shrines to her at home, as well as worshipping her at the temple (usually on a Friday). Most often, she appears as a beautiful woman with four arms standing in a lotus flower. This is how she first appears in the Hindu epics, during an episode in which the gods of good battle demons for the elixir of eternal life.

Vishnu's protection of the world—and Brahma's continuing re-creation of it—cannot exist without a "destroyer." This is Shiva, another blue-bodied god in human form, who is usually depicted with a third eye and a cobra necklace. Shiva is often a man, but is sometimes represented as half-man, half-woman. Known sometimes as the "Lord of the Dance," Shiva's Dance of Death is intended to destroy the world. He is usually accompanied by the Mother Goddess, Devi. She is described in many stories—sometimes as Kali, the goddess of death, or Sati, the goddess of marital fidelity and fecundity—but mostly, she is represented as his devoted wife for all eternity, Parvati.

Brahma, the four-headed, four-armed, swan-riding first god of the *trimurti* is rarely seen in images. In fact, there are only two temples devoted to him in the whole of India.

Gods and Deities

One of the most common images in India is that of Lord Ganesh, or Ganesa. A human form, but with an elephant's head, he is the son of Shiva and Parvati, and is regarded as the Helper, the Remover of Obstacles. He is also considered the patron of travelers.

The case of Krishna is confusing; the greatest warrior, the ideal man—not to mention an umbrella term for hundreds of other of deities that bear his name. The best-known representations of Krishna show him as a dark-skinned, good-looking hero of culture and learning, as well as a strong warrior. Nobody, not even Hindu scholars, seems sure which character he is—which might explain why one of his nicknames is "the Trickster God."

The same is true of (Sri) Rama, another *avatar*, or incarnation, of Lord Vishnu. He is the hero of the great Indian martial epic, the *Ramayana*—a kind of subcontinental *Odyssey*—which has also found its way into the mythologies of the Far East. His image is not seen that often, but usually reflects the personal taste of the image's creator.

Other gods, goddesses, and deities that pervade the lives of ordinary Hindus include the river goddess Ganga, and the god of day and night—and of cosmic justice—Varuna (in later scriptures he is called the Lord of the Waters).

Buddha also has his place among Indian deities, although this is largely due to an attempt to assimilate Buddha into a Hindu worldview, after Buddhism was effectively driven out of India by the 13th century. Indeed, the Buddha in the Hindu pantheon is not the same Buddha known in the West, merely a borrowed name and character.

Left: The first to feel the rays of sunlight each morning, the Sun Temple in Konark, is an important site of worship in India.

Below: These caves served as important places of worship for Jain ascetics.

Gods and Deities

Buddhism and Monasteries

Buddhism, according to most scholars, began in India in the 4th century BC with the birth of Siddhartha Gautama, a rich prince who renounced his life of privilege for religious contemplation and enlightenment through advanced meditation techniques. According to legend, it was under a tree in the forests of Gaya (now Bihar) that Gautama pondered the mystery of existence, before expressing the wisdom he found there as the Four Noble Truths. These were the following: all of life is suffering; the cause of suffering is desire; the end of desire leads to the end of suffering; and desire can be suppressed through meditation. By then, Gautama had

become the Lord Buddha, and he spent the rest of his days acquiring disciples throughout India. For nearly 1500 years, India was the world center of Buddhism. But, with the incursion of Western invaders, and the spread of Islam from the 7th century onwards, Buddhism found itself increasingly marginalized. The rise of Hinduism did not help either, and, in the end, Buddhism was restricted to the fringes of India. Royalty switched its allegiance to Hindu intellectual and philosophical endeavors. Interestingly, though, the growth of Hindu monastic communities showed signs of having been strongly influenced by the scholarly traditions of Buddhism.

Only more recently, in the 20th century, has Buddhism shown any signs of a large-scale revival in India beyond its traditional heartlands.

The revival of Buddhism was probably helped by a growing interest in Buddhist philosophy in the West during the 19th century and the efforts of archaeologists and antiquarians. They are the ones who rediscovered many of India's long-neglected Buddhist treasures. Such research has also shown the cross-fertilization between Buddhist and Hindu ideals of religious architecture. Just as Hindu architects borrowed from the Jains (another Indian religious faith) and Muslims from both Hindus and Jains, so the Buddhists borrowed

Below: The numerous religious sites that fill India's landscape illustrate the importance of religion to the people of this diverse country.
Right: The image of the seated Buddha is common to Buddhist temples.

Gods and Deities

Far Left and Center: Prayer Wheels are a typical feature of Buddhist architecture.

Bottom Right: Statues of the golden Buddha fill religious temples, especially in northern India on the border between Nepal and Tibet.

from Hindus. These reflect common philosophical backgrounds. Furthermore, local variations—type of stone used, for example—means that one cannot easily speak of a single style of Indian Buddhist architecture. Given the time span over which Buddhism developed—it was preeminent for a thousand years and more—it was probably inevitable that changes would occur.

The monuments to Indian Buddhism still visible today include the remains from the once-thriving Buddhist centre of Harwan, a 3rd-century complex in the state of Jammu and Kashmir. The sculpted and decorative tiles that survive from the *stupa* at Harwan display a wide range of motifs. Some of these are figurative, others abstract. They include warriors on horseback, dancers, minstrels, flowers, vines, and birds.

In the Bhagalpur region, splendid rock carvings depict a variety of Hindu deities, proving how close the links could be between the two faiths. These hail from the Gupta period (4th-7th century AD) and originate from the sites of Bhagalpur and Sultanganj in Bihar. More, older cave decorations

can be seen at Ajanta. These date back to the 2nd and 1st centuries BC, when Buddhism was still in its infancy. The great Gupta Empire of the 6th century saw these decorations enhanced with paintings and further carvings.

Sadly, many of these relics are now just fragments, but museums in India still house fine collections of Buddhist carvings and decorations. These include the remains of the great Bharhut *stupa* on show in the Kolkata Museum and the 2nd century *stupa* of Amravati in the museum at Chennai.

The Mahabodhi temple at Bodhgaya, where the Buddha first gained enlightenment at the age of 29, is one of the main centers of monastic Buddhist learning in India today. Its origins are unclear, with some sources suggesting that the great Buddhist monarch Ashoka constructed it in the 3rd century BC. Others, meanwhile, give a much later date.

For all the trials and tribulations Buddhism has been through in India—from state religion to obscure sect—it is remarkable that so much has survived for so long.

Animals in Religion

Left: Elephants are one of many important animals in Indian culture and feature in many festivals and rituals.

Center: Lord Ganesh is often represented as a human with the head of an elephant.

Bottom Right: Regal and majestic, the tiger is both revered and feared in India.

Given the importance of religion in Indian life, it is perhaps not surprising that many religious beliefs, traditions, and festivals encompass animals as well. Ancient Indian scriptures such as the *Upanishads* and the *Garudapurana* include detailed writings on animals such as horses and cattle, as well as philosophical teachings that use examples from the animal world to illustrate abstract concepts.

Hinduism, the most widely followed religion in India, teaches the notion of *ahimsa*, a Sanskrit word meaning non-violence. Hindus believe that all animals should be treated well. Cows are regarded as sacred in Hinduism (giving rise to the expression "sacred cow") and cannot be killed in India. Thus cows can often be seen wandering through villages and towns with scant regard for any disruption they cause to traffic! No devout Hindu will eat beef.

Some Hindu deities have strong associations with animals. For example, the elephant-headed god Ganesh is sometimes depicted riding on the back of a giant mouse. Illustrations from India's history often depict other deities being transported by animals such as peacocks, cows, or elephants.

Buddhists, followers of another of India's great religions, try to avoid harming any living thing. Some of the first animal hospitals in the world were founded by Buddhists to ease the pain and suffering of sick and injured animals.

Jains avoid eating all meat because they abhor the killing of animals for any reason. Particularly devout Jain monks will even wear face masks or veils in order to avoid accidentally killing insects by breathing them in or swallowing them! This is viewed in accordance with Jains' reverence for all life.

Cattle are important in Indian life for many reasons.

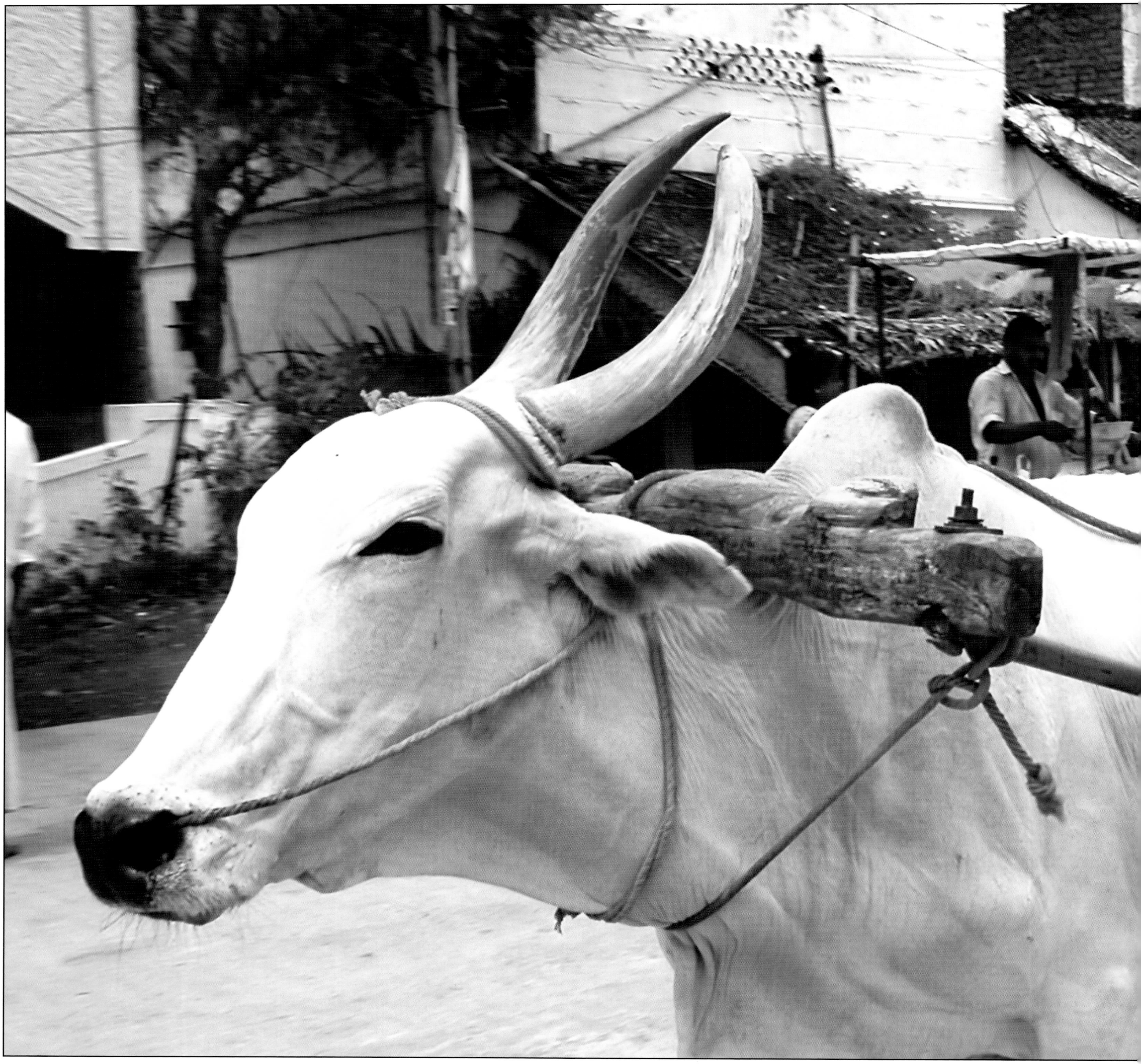

Diversity

Rural versus Urban

Life in the Indian countryside has always been tough, even grueling. A farmer or craftsman would work many long hours in either baking sun or pouring rain, for little more than the possibility of feeding his family. For countless generations, migration to cities has appeared an attractive option to those whose circumstances—social or financial—made staying in rural India impossible.

The trend accelerated after the great influenza epidemic of 1918. This affected most of the world, but it hit the Indian population particularly hard, with tens of millions dying from the virus. In response to such losses, the population expanded enormously, and the land could scarcely cope; many decided to opt for city life instead. This caused problems within the cities, of course.

As a result, shanties (or *basti*) proliferated around all of India's major cities. These varied from a few rickety lean-tos made out of whatever material was to hand, to enormous settlements built along railroad tracks, around factories, and along riverbanks.

Cities often became the victims of their own success; the larger they grew, the more likely they were to attract immigrants from impoverished rural areas that had been devastated by famine, flood, or disease. This put extraordinary and intolerable pressure on urban authorities' capabilities to provide sanitation, safe drinking water, and basic amenities.

Worst off were those who had no permanent accommodation at all. Even today, as India's cities develop and expand at an astonishing rate, the urban poor are still alarmingly visible.

However, the process seems unstoppable; the richer India's cities become, the greater their pull on those in the countryside. Within a decade, Bombay is set to become the fourth-largest metropolitan area on earth. It is to be hoped that the riches brought by economic expansion will enable all city dwellers to share in the new prosperity of a 21st century nation, and that the journey from rural poverty to a new life in town will not be the disappointment it has so often been in the past.

Left and Below: The gap between rural and urban India is growing faster than ever and affects all who live in this large country.

Villages

India's official census regards settlements with fewer than 5,000 inhabitants as villages, and estimates that there may be more than half a million such settlements throughout the subcontinent. These, of course, range from a few mud huts with bulrush roofs to a thriving settlement of modern buildings built of brick, steel, and concrete. There may be a building housing the village council; a few modest shops; maybe a public radio hooked up to loudspeakers, and even a guesthouse (or *dharamshala*).

But it is hard to argue that this is where India's basic cultural values flourish most of all. India's population is still largely an agricultural one, and even those who have lived in cities for generations still have a family link with the land. The timeless image of the Indian village is that of bent-backed farmers driving bullock-drawn plows through muddy fields, women in saris with water pitchers on their heads, mud huts, oxen, and happy children. It is a romanticized view. India has changed. It has been industrialized, and now has booming computer and electronics industries. Village life is regarded as a guardian of the old certainties, even if it sometimes means the most terrible poverty, suffering, and hunger—especially for the "untouchable" castes of society.

These untouchables, or *dalits*, rarely live within a village, and yet they almost never have settlements of their own. They live in a kind of no-man's-land between villages. In truth, the relationship between villages is often complicated in India. Thousands of villages are linked by relationships that are familial, economic, or political. Even within a single village, there is more than a simple nucleus of houses. Indeed, there can be as many as forty different social castes in one village, for example.

The differences in the makeup of villages are usually dependent on an assortment of factors. In different parts of the subcontinent, ownership of land can vary between high castes and middle castes. Some higher caste landowners till their own fields, while others buy in local laborers.

Topography means that villages often fit different patterns. In hilly areas, the buildings are more dispersed, as they are in the "wet" states of West Bengal and Kerala. Indeed, in the latter, villages are often built in rows along lanes or roads, and it is sometimes difficult for a traveler to know where one village ends and another begins.

There has been a notable decline in the number of traditional artisans in Indian villages over the last half-century. Oil-pressers, blacksmiths, woodcarvers, and weavers are diminishing in number. This is partly due to an increase in

Right: Village life in India has become more diverse than in the past, yet agriculture and farming remain strong features of the rural landscape.

Far Right: Agriculture is a key aspect of Indian rural life.

Colorful glassware is just one of the many crafts that exist in India.

Villages

Left: The colorful door of a typical rural Indian mud house.

Below: Villagers are often poor and rely upon hard work and tenacity to survive.

migration away from traditional village life as more people seek better-paid work in cities. From Kerala, for example, thousands of villagers emigrate for months at a time to work in the Persian Gulf.

But, for many millions of Indians, the bonds with the countryside remain strong. They remember the sense of civic pride that all Indian villages have, even in times of hardship. They remember above all the strong work ethic that prevails in many villages—a work ethic that has often enabled them to overcome the tough times. They remember the weddings and the rite-of-passage celebrations. They remember the local rituals and traditions that make them what they are. All these, for many Indians, spring from the village where they, their parents, or their grandparents were born. Even if it is thousands of miles away—right across the country—it will remain with them for always.

36194 डब्ल्यू·डी·एस6

Railways in India

Most tourists, if they travel by rail in India, do not experience the crowded, sometimes hilarious, sometimes dangerous, reality of rail travel in the country. Western subway systems, and the commuters that use them, do not even come close when it comes to numbers. It is still quite common to witness sights—familiar 30 years ago—of travelers squatting on the roofs of trains and hanging from doors. It is also still possible to travel behind giant steam locomotives and to revel in the luxury of the Raj on a new generation of special hotel trains crisscrossing India.

Indian Railways really began in 1853, encouraged by British colonists, who ensured they had big financial interests in this new means of travel. It opened up the economic possibilities of their new Indian property. After all, India was a rich country, and railways could help run the Empire and transport its riches faster.

The first train ran in Maharashtra state, from Bori Bunder to Thana via Bombay (Mumbai). By 1880, main lines were thrusting into the country from the ports of Mumbai, Madras, and Calcutta.

In 1947, the network was nationalized. Although it is currently being privatized, there are still 40,000 miles (64,300 km) of railways in this mighty country, supporting 8,702 trains. Sikkim, the remote Himalayan kingdom, is the only state not connected to the Indian Railways system. Five billion rail journeys are undertaken annually, mostly in and around major population centers such as Kolkata and Delhi.

Carrying the cargo of India's precious natural resources is still important, and almost anything that can be carried by rail is carried by rail from steel to fertilizer, from fish to camel milk. An efficiency drive is underway to improve the punctuality of cargo trains.

But the rustic and rural nature of India's railway backwaters is also still one of the country's greatest attractions for travelers and railway enthusiasts alike. The little Darjeeling-Himalaya railway winds up through the Himalayan foothills, going through tea plantations and forests, around impossibly tight bends on a rickety 2-foot-6-inch-wide (75 cm) track. The Nilgiri Mountain Railway is a similarly beautiful and unforgettable trek up steep gradients in ancient coaches pulled by ancient steam engines.

Looking out the window, from the wooden bench inside the steam from the smokestack mingling with the forest mist it is easy to understand that the romance of India is just as present in its railways as it is in the Taj Mahal or the Red Fort.

Cities

The South

Chennai, formerly Madras, is the capital of Tamil Nadu state and is known as India's "Gateway to the South." With a population of six million, it is one of India's ten most densely-populated urban areas. Its beginnings were modest. Indeed, it was nothing more than a fishing port, Madraspatnam, founded in 1639.

The city is similar to Bombay in its relative cosmopolitanism. The city prides itself on being the artistic hub of southern India's arts and crafts, from music to sculpture. If Bombay is the center of Bollywood, northern India's movie industry, then Chennai is most certainly the heart of the lesser-known, but still influential, southern Indian studios.

In Karnataka state, Bangalore is doing its best to keep pace with Chennai. It may not have the larger city's grace and history and some say its drive for modernization is at the cost of its character but what a bustling place it is. Probably one of the fastest-growing cities in the whole of Asia, it is recognized as the capital of India's computer industry.

India's other "Silicon Valley" is located in crowded Hyderabad. It was originally founded by Quli Qutub Shah in 1512 as a fortress city called Golconda.

Close links with the British East India Company, and a succession of important rulers, led to Hyderabad gaining a reputation as a city of architectural variety and great style. Here, Mogul, Colonial, and Indo-Saracenic forms seem to meld very easily together.

India's southern and eastern coasts were among the first to be settled by Westerners. With India's technological revolution gaining ground, and the southern cities also waking up to the tourist riches at their disposal if not ancient temples, then glorious sandy beaches these could once again be among India's greatest attractions for the foreign visitor.

Bottom Left: India's main cities remain one of the country's primary tourist attractions.

Right: This southern Indian city illustrates the growing urbanization of India.

Motorized rickshaws are common in major cities like Bombay.

Cities

Bombay/Mumbai

Left: Sport is a popular pastime for the residents of India's major cities.
Below: One of the many sights in India's cities
Bottom Right: A typical urban street scene.

Westerners often assume that Mumbai (formerly Bombay) is India's capital. That honor, of course, is New Delhi's, but as many a native of Mumbai will patiently explain, it might seem a little weird. After all, Mumbai is larger, more populated, and more prosperous. It is the subcontinent's financial and commercial hub, and it is India at its most dynamic and modern.

Rather like New York, Mumbai city occupies a series of islands off the Konkan coast in Maharashtra state. The immense overcrowding of the city which, during the hot summer months can make conditions on the sidewalks very hot, humid, and unpleasant has led to a new Mumbai establishing itself on the mainland. And it continues to grow. The population of the city (not counting its suburbs) in the 1995 census was 13 million, making it one of the largest and certainly one of the most densely populated settlements on the planet.

Mumbai's street life reflects this. Its infrastructure, both road and rail-based, is light years ahead of most other Indian cities, and yet the roads are still jammed with private taxis, *tuk-tuks*, trucks, and buses, not to mention cars.

Mumbai's status as a major port has helped it grow as a cultured and cosmopolitan city, and it is usually named as one of the Western tourist's favorite Indian city destinations. Perhaps Mumbai's most celebrated, recent gift to the world is the dazzlingly enjoyable world of Bollywood movies. The extravagant, all-singing, all-dancing movie genre has now become one of the major features of the city. In fact, it is becoming a tourist attraction in itself not least because generations of expatriate Indians, devoted to the form, flock here to worship at the cinematic shrine.

Diversity
Wildlife

If all human life can be found in India, it is just as true that the subcontinent's wildlife is immensely rich and varied. This has much to do with India's many different habitats, landscapes, and climates. Much of the country is covered with forests from the subtropical jungles of the Andaman Islands and the hills of the Western Ghats to the conifer forests of the Himalayas.

Incredibly, India is home to 7.6 percent of the world's mammal species, 12.6 percent of its birdlife, and 6.2 percent of all reptiles. Yet, surprisingly, only a relatively small number of these creatures are native to India. The prehistoric collision of the Indian landmass with the Himalayas wiped out many indigenous species, which were replaced by animals and reptiles then crossing from Asia through the mountains towards the south.

The native species include varieties of peacock, as well as curious rarities such as the Nilgiri Leaf monkey, and the carmine and brown Beddome's toads, found in the Western Ghats. Both these species are under threat, although neither has the public fame and renown of the most iconic of India's animals: the tiger.

Although most people would associate India with the elephant, its most majestic and sought-after animal is without question the tiger. Feared and admired for both its muscular grace and lethal hunting powers, its habitat has shrunk, and the incessant growth of India's population has meant that it has come increasingly into conflict with encroaching humanity. This has resulted in scores of fatal tiger attacks; and while the animal was hunted for sport in the days of the British

Raj, today many tigers are shot simply to protect villagers in remote areas who have strayed into the tiger's domain.

Among other animals common to India are antelope, bison, leopard, hyena, and game birds of every description.

After decades of neglect, India's national parks and conservation areas are being expanded by the government. The prestigious Project Tiger has been set up to fight against the continued problem of tiger poaching. There are 500 wildlife sanctuaries and 14 biosphere reserves, four of which are part of the World Network of Biosphere Reserves. With so much money flooding in from tourism often safari tourism it seems that India has woken up and is putting a stop to the exploitation of one of its most colorful and alluring assets.

Wildlife is a main tourist attraction, and safaris are a popular way to see some of India's exotic animals.

Cows

India is a predominantly agricultural country, and even if the Hindu religion did not venerate the cow to the extent that it does, there is no doubt that the animal would have a tremendous importance to the rural folk of the subcontinent. Indeed, its usefulness has probably helped the animal's status as a source of life and therefore something to be praised and honored.

Cows, after all, give birth to bulls, and enable the cycle of agriculture and subsistence. It is the bull that is yoked to the plow to till the fields and paddies, and that provides transportation to market and town.

Cows produce milk, from which the locals produce the health-giving yogurt. This yogurt is then churned to produce butter, which can be converted into the clarified butter called *ghee*, a staple of cooking in both rural and urban India and also regarded as an elixir. Cows' milk is also used in the manufacture of homemade candies and desserts such as *paneer*, *khoya*, and *mana*, as well as cottage cheese and buttermilk.

More unusual to the Western palate, cows' urine, or *gau mutra*, is an important part of Ayurveda, the ancient Hindu system of medicine although it is most commonly used as a disinfectant or to treat skin rashes and diseases.

More important still is the famous *gobar*, or cow dung. Many mud huts are made from an amalgam of *gobar* and plaster, which, it is believed, keeps insects and reptiles away. This is also the reason why so many earthenware storage pots for grains and pulses are made of the same substance. *Gobar* can fuel kitchen fires and, according to ecologists, is an environmentally friendly fertilizer.

Many Hindus believe that the spirit of Lakshmi, the goddess of wealth, is to be found in *gobar*. This religious angle finds expression less in the creation of carved and graven images in great temples and shrines, and more in popular festivals all over India the greatest being the thunderous *Gopashtami*. Hindu fire rituals, or *havan*, have the cow as their centerpiece, and tribute is paid to the animal in the form of milk, yogurt, *ghee*, *gobar*, and *gau mutra*. It is not too great a claim to say that many Hindus love the cow. There are even charitable foundations to look after old, lame, or orphaned cows wandering the streets or the countryside, notably the *Gaushala*, or "House of the Cow." Go to any cow fair in any part of India and there will be cows for sale, not to mention a bewildering array of cow jewelry to beautify the farmer's favorite beast.

Mahatma Gandhi wrote that the innocence in the eyes of cows was a message to humanity—that we were put on the Earth, by the creator, not to destroy animals, but to protect them.

Left: As a predominately agricultural society, India holds the cow in high esteem.
Right: One of India's most revered animals, is the cow plays an essential role in religion and Ayurvedic medicine.

Camels

Ships of the Western Deserts

Left: The Pushkar camel fair in Rajasthan is one of the world's largest livestock markets.
Below: The camel is the emblem of Rajasthan.

The camel is one of the symbols of the great deserts of Rajasthan province in western India. It is one of the toughest yet also most graceful animals in the world, capable of storing water and fat in its body (although not, as most people think, in the humps) for weeks at a time to survive under the burning desert sun. For the rest of the world, camel trains have become synonymous with desert travel, and the animal is so important to Rajasthanis that it is the emblem of the state. Camels have the ability to work hard in very high temperatures of 93°F–105°F (34°C–41°C). Above this, their shaggy coats make them sweat and lose valuable water supplies. They can also happily snack on thorny desert plants that enable them to keep fueled throughout a journey. In

ancient times, the use of these great animals in long merchant "trains" took all kinds of Indian goods—silks, gold, spices—to the Middle and Near East, and eventually to Europe.

Camels are also prized for their dairy products, which were a valuable resource for the men and merchants who crossed the deserts with them. It is much richer in protein than cows' milk, and the milk can also be made into camel butter. In India, yogurt made from camels' milk is regarded not only as a delicacy but also as a health product.

The Pushkar camel fair in Rajasthan is considered not only one of India's greatest but also one of the world's biggest livestock markets. The Pushkar fair is organized by the Raikas the caste of camel-breeders—proud, orange-turbaned men who

inhabit the dusty and dry surrounding hills. In November 2004, some 50,000 camels a tenth of the entire camel population were brought to market here.

There are concerns, however, that the camel's habitat could be under threat. The Raikas are reluctant to give up their traditional habits, which, some ecologists say, could be leading to over-grazing of a region already affected by drought and raising the threat of a dustbowl. But others point to the possibility of all-new grazing lands opening up along the Gandhi Canal, which brings water from the Punjab to irrigate the great Thar Desert of Rajasthan. With a new diet, and a new but familiar habitat, the future of India's camels could yet be secure.

Elephants

The Indian elephant's Latin name is *Elephas maximus indicus*, and it is a subspecies of the Asian Elephant. It can also be found in neighboring countries such as Bhutan, Bangladesh, Myanmar, and Nepal.

These gentle giants, sometimes growing up to 32 feet (10 m) in length, are hardly ever found in the wild. They roam and forage through jungle territory, rarely staying in one settlement for any length of time.

However, India boasts thousands of elephants in captivity. This is probably due to the religious significance of the elephant—the god Ganesh has an elephant's head—and for their usefulness as domestic animals. Many work in timber yards owing to their immense strength. Kerala, in southern India, has 700 elephants in captivity, and these are often treated with extravagant respect. They are revered, groomed, and given a high rank in society.

Most Keralan religious festivals feature either real elephants or effigies of elephants. These events include the *Arattupuzha Pooram*, the *Chinakkathoor Pooram*, and *Trichur Pooram*. During the festivals, people are festooned with beautifully colorful and ornate ceremonial wear, and carry images of the deity around the temples. Elephants are dressed with gold necklaces and bells.

The Guruyayur Temple in Kerala owns more than 60 domesticated elephants, and devotees have even built an Elephant Palace a few miles away in Punnathur Kotta. The daily ceremonial rounds at the Keralan Koodalmanikyam Temple feature no fewer than 17 elephants, seven of which sport headdresses made of solid gold; the other 10 have to make do with pure silver.

Elephants are cared for by a special caste called *mahouts*, and each elephant has three mahouts to guard its welfare. In the Malayalam language, these mahouts are called *pappam*. Their most important duty is to keep the ceremonial elephants in good condition, which they achieve by bathing and massaging the elephant's hide with small rocks and coconut husks. During the monsoon season, mahouts have even been known to use Ayurvedic rejuvenation techniques on the elephants with decoctions and infusions of herbs.

Far Left: Despite the elephant appearing in images all over India, the animal is rarely found in the wild.
Left: Most elephants in India are domesticated and are put to work hauling huge weights.

Cared for by a special caste called the *mahouts*, the elephant is revered and very well treated.

Rhinoceros

The Jungle

Schoolbooks call it the *Rhinoceros unicornis*. In the primitive, dark green undergrowth of the northern Indian hills, on the border with Nepal and the Himalayas, these enormous and respected creatures lead a peaceful and solitary existence. Despite their strict vegetarian diet, they weigh up to 6,000 lb (2,720 kg), are 6 feet (1.8 m) tall and 12.5 feet (3.8 m) long. The single horn on its snout can grow up to 2 feet (60 cm) long. Usually they shy away from humans, but if hungry they may wander into a remote village in search of food. They appear clumsy, with a tough hide like rusting and riveted steel and the gentle eyes of a cow. But, when disturbed they will charge, and these attacks have been known to be fatal.

They are among the few colonies of rhinos left in Asia other colonies, of a slightly different species, are located in Java and Sumatra in the East Indies. They are also the world's only amphibious rhinos, and as such, they enjoy basking in cool rivers and grazing on aquatic grasses in the sun.

Rhinos are in danger of extinction all over the world, but particularly on the African subcontinent. There, the long-held belief that rhino horn powder is an aphrodisiac has led to widespread poaching of wild rhinos.

The Indian government, however, has taken steps to preserve the country's rhinos. From a figure of around 200, nearly 50 years ago, the wild rhino population of India has increased to around 2,500. Poachers, however, are still stalking the animals, and it is a full-time job for conservation agencies on both sides of the India-Nepal border to safeguard this ancient inhabitant of India's jungles. If successful, the program will ensure that these majestic, old tough-skinned animals will continue to haunt the remote northern floodplains of India.

Bottom Left: In grave danger of extinction, the rhinoceros is another animal that the government and animal rights organizations are working to protect.

Right: Shy and vegetarian, these animals can be fatal to humans if they charge.

Snakes

Cultural Significance

It may seem strange to outsiders that Hindus revere snakes when the subcontinent contains some of the world's deadliest examples. Best-known of all Indian snakes is the aggressive king cobra with its venomous bite. There are thought to be another 50 or so poisonous snakes in India, and the subcontinent is also home to one of the longest and strongest of the world's snakes, the reticulated python, which can grow up to 32 feet (10 m) in length. The cobra and python are timid and are therefore rarely seen in urban areas. On the other hand, the saw-scaled viper and Russell's viper are common near human settlements and they are dangerous for this reason.

So why the fascination with an animal that can kill? Everyone knows the famous images of snake charmers and fakirs sitting cross-legged on sidewalks in India's major cities, apparently "charming" a snake to dance out of a little wicker pot to the hypnotic tune of a reed pipe. This is not quite what it seems, however. The snakes have had their poisonous fangs removed and are often drugged. But the spectacle almost always draws a crowd, of locals and baffled foreigners alike.

Snake worship is one of the most colorful and exotic of India's cultural practices. It has deep roots in the Hindu beliefs of millions of Indians. There is only one animal thought to be holier than the snake, the cow. Many Hindus offer gifts of eggs and milk to their snake gods on *Nag Panchami*, or serpent festival. In Hindu mythology, there are eight notable snake figures. These include Shesha,

a snake with 1,000 heads, who supports the weight of the world and who sheltered Lord Krishna from a thunderstorm when he was born. The better-known Kaliya was an evil, five-headed, river-dwelling demon-god snake that terrorized the Brahma in his childhood, until the god Krishna danced on Kaliya's heads and subdued him.

Vasuki's tail stirred the oceans into the ambrosia of immortality. The world is encircled by an endless snake, Ananta, while Manasadevi is the snake queen. Padmanhaba is a snake that is said to be the guardian of the southern states of India. It is no accident that the famed Indian snake-boat races take place in Kerala, which is also the location of the fabulous Sarpakkavu caves home to the snake gods.

There are close associations between snakes and both the supreme gods Vishnu and Shiva. The latter traditionally carries a snake across his chest. Snake worship is generally more important in southern India, and worship of Shiva is more common there than that of Vishnu. Often exquisite shrines are built in honor of the snake gods, and worshippers bring offerings of flowers and candles. Sometimes, people build their own tiny snake-god shrines in their gardens or in front of their houses. Such shrines can often be found under the *neem* tree, whose leaves are thought to heal snakebites. Legend has it that killing a snake intentionally will lead to death, and that snakes, angered by insult or disrespect, can place curses on those who have abused them, leading to possible sickness and misfortune.

Far Left: The King Cobra is one of India's most famous indigenous snakes.
Top: Trees that take the shape of snakes, such as this one, are considered sacred.
Bottom: Snake worship has Hindu roots and remains popular today.

The snake charmers of India remove the cobras' dangerous fangs and any possibility of a fatal bite.

Diversity

People

In a country of a billion people, spread over such a vast landmass and in all types of climate and topography, how does one even begin to explain and rationalize the variety of its population? By religion? There are scores of religious faiths. By language? There are 18 different official languages in India and hundreds of dialects. Racial groupings are just as difficult, since India has been subject to hundreds of invasions and migrations in its history.

Perhaps the most relevant means of investigating population diversity in India today is to remember how fast the country is changing and modernizing. A little over a century ago, most Indians were illiterate farm laborers; now the country is experiencing enormous urban population growth, and new sectors of economic activity are springing up every month. This is changing the way people live and work

For most Indians, income remains low by Western standards. About two-thirds of them still work the land. Standards of literacy remain painfully low, despite repeated attempts by state and federal government to rectify this through numerous education programs.

It is in the countryside where the caste system is still most prevalent. It is an article of Hindu faith, yet this system in which one's social standing is determined by the caste level of one's family is also practiced by adherents of other faiths. From the priestly Brahmans down to the lowliest *dalits*, or untouchables, the caste system has persisted in India. Some say that, in a country where income and livelihood can often be precarious, it is a way of belonging to a secure social group.

In the villages and fields, traditions die hard: arranged marriages are commonplace, the role of women is subservient, and religious orthodoxy often holds sway. Kinship networks bind families and villages closely together. If a bride is abused by her husband when she moves away to his village, for example, it is a question of honor not just for the bride's immediate family but also for her whole community.

Three-quarters of India's population still stick to these time-honored principles, although such is the rate of growth of the subcontinent's cities that the urban-rural balance is shifting and fast.

One-fifth of India's gigantic labor force is now involved not in farming, handicraft, or "country ways" but in the organized sector. This means employment in an industry such as quarrying or the railways. It means taking up an official government job in the post office or in healthcare. There are modern utilities, a service sector, and commerce. All this means leaving behind not just a traditional way of doing things but also familiar surroundings, and organizing one's life along new paths. It means moving to large population centers, and picking up urban habits. The expansion of India's urban environment has weakened links with the past, critics say. How else to explain the phenomenon of Bollywood cinema, of the Indian software revolution, and of non-arranged, "love marriages" among the growing numbers of educated and well-paid middle-class Indians? As India's economy changes, so its people are changing.

India has made enormous strides towards prosperity in the last century. Yet, by Western standards, it remains slow in many ways, levels of Indian productivity are still low, education is often basic, and old habits die hard. But, while some things may not change, new trends—just as fascinating and complex as the ones they are replacing—are becoming visible among India's human throng.

Left and Bottom: The people of today's India are a diverse mixture of traditional and modern, a gap often felt between generations.

133

The North

Sikhism

The Punjab, in the northwest of India, is mostly a gently sloping plain with a subtropical climate that varies between arid and humid. Bordering it to the north and west, however, are high, rugged mountain passes. Punjab, then, offers both a fertile and a desert face to the world.

It is also home to the majority of India's Sikhs, one of the country's and now one of the world's greatest religions. It is also one of the world's youngest faiths. It is therefore ironic that one of the Western stereotypes of India is the colorful turban, or *patka*, worn by practicing Sikhs when, in reality, they comprise only a fraction of the subcontinent's population.

The faith began in southern India in Tamil Nadu among followers of the Hindu Vaishnava Bhakti movement, which is based on the worship of the god Vishnu. It gradually spread northwards. At its heart was a rejection of the rigid hierarchy of Hindu society especially its caste system but it also drew on the benign teachings of the mystical Sufi cult of Islam.

The chief figure of Sikhism is Guru Nanak, who was born in 1469. A great enthusiast of this hybrid new faith, he set out on four sacred journeys across India after having a vision, in which God told him to preach the word to all mankind. He built a temple in Kartarpur (in modern-day Pakistan), which became an important pilgrimage site.

The ruling Mogul emperors of India had been tolerant of faiths other than Islam, but they found the rise of Sikhism worrying. Guru Nanak's successors to the leadership of the faith were dealt with harshly, but in 1699, the guru Gobind Rai (1675–1708) baptized five Sikhs into a fraternity called the Pure Ones, or *khalsa*. They were given the name *Singh* (meaning "lion"), which was to be shared by all Sikhs as a matter of religious solidarity (all Sikh women share the name *kaur*, or "princess"). The Sikhs organized themselves again, this time as a tribe of soldier-saints, dedicated to preserving their faith and worshipping their god. At first, the *khalsa* appeared weak in the face of Mogul power, but early in the 18th century, Persian invaders helped undermine the western Mogul Empire, and the Sikhs moved back onto the plains of the Punjab and set down roots.

After some initial, bloody clashes with the British in the first and second Sikh wars of the mid-19th century, relations with the Raj improved. But India's independence in 1947 saw the removal of all privileges granted by the British to religious minorities. It also isolated many Sikh farmers who had left rich estates in Pakistan to return to their Punjabi homelands. Increasing Sikh militancy resulted in the disastrous attack by Indian government forces on the fabulous Golden Temple of Amritsar in 1984. The holiest of Sikh shrines was desecrated and many people died.

For Sikhs, the Hindu cycle of birth, death, and rebirth is accepted. There is one god, and he is formless, timeless, without name, and unknowable by mankind. Worshipping images of God is forbidden. All creatures are equal in His eye. In Sikh society, the Hindu caste system is rejected, and there is no priesthood. There is a fixed class system, but this is more visible in rural areas than in towns and cities.

A peculiar feature of the religion is a devotion to the concept of the five Ks or five emblems of the *khalsa*. The first four are *kangha* ("comb"), *kacch* ("military trousers"), *kirpan* ("sabre"), and *kara* ("bracelet of steel"). Yet, the most important is *kesa* ("hair"). This must remain unshorn for life, and a khalsa who loses his hair is regarded as a *patit*, or renegade. This explains the elaborate turban headdress, which has come to define the Sikh to the rest of the world.

Below: Home to Sikhs, northern India contains some beautiful examples of temple architecture.

Right: The Punjab region is home to the majority of India's Sikhs.

The turban, or *patka*, worn by Sikhs is available in a range of vibrant colors.

The West

Rajasthan

Rajasthan was once known as Rajputana, or the land of the Rajputs, and it has long been regarded in India and abroad as one of the glories of the subcontinent. It is a land of great contrasts and immense historical importance. It is also home to some of the most mesmerizing buildings in the whole of India.

Rajput literally means "son of a king." It was the Rajputs, living on the border of the newly Islamicized Persia, who bravely resisted initial Muslim incursions into India beginning in the 7th century AD. Although some Rajput kings and princes did pay homage to the Delhi Sultanate and the Mogul rulers of later centuries, the Rajputs always represented an independent Hindu outpost. Even today, nearly 90 percent of the population of Rajasthan is Hindu although Muslim influences, especially in the arts, are often recognizable.

The Islamic invaders not always bent on outright conquest came out of the wild and sandy wastelands of the Great Indian Desert, to the north and west of modern Rajasthan. The local name is the Thar Desert, or "place of the dead." As the traveler moves southeast across Rajasthan, the land becomes more forgiving and less barren, although the badlands along the Chambal River are as bleak as any landscape in all of India.

There is some fertile land in Rajasthan, but it is mainly a dry area, and the people and animals are hardy. So it is hardly surprising, then, that most of India's camels live in this state. Housing conditions are primitive, with most village and farm dwellings consisting of one room, with no windows or ventilation; the walls are made of mud, and the roofs of rushes. These farmers, if they are fortunate enough to live in the fertile southeastern corner of Rajasthan, usually grow wheat, barley, sugar, or legumes for a living. The state is also a large producer of edible oils. Rajasthan farmers are a resourceful group, cultivating crops in the driest, most unfavorable conditions even up to the edges of the Thar Desert.

These agricultural settlements are rare, yet they always offer a stark contrast to the often unbelievable splendor and elegance of the dwellings of the Rajput ruling classes. Their forts and palaces are covered in detail elsewhere, but it is impossible not to mention them when discussing the wealth of Rajasthan. The Rajputs were and are proud of their reputation as fearless defenders of their land. Their passion for building forts and the pride they showed in making them as impregnable as they are beautiful is proved time and again in cities like Jaipur and Udaipur, not to mention remoter places like Jaisalmer.

Rajasthan is modernizing, and quarrying and mining are making their economic presence felt. The state produces India's entire output of lead and zinc, as well as emeralds, garnets, gypsum, and silver ore. The Chambal Valley project is an ambitious plan to provide the state not only with electricity but also with a freshwater irrigation system. The water will be channeled from the Punjab, 400 miles (644 km) to the north, to Rajasthan's driest regions via the Indira Gandhi canal.

But Rajasthanis are also deeply attached to their traditions. Traditional arts and crafts have a special place here, and prized items include tie-dye, block, and Baguru printing and Zari embroidery. There are many religious festivals, and although many people are devout Hindus, they know how to have a good time. Never more so, perhaps, than during the amazing Gangor festival, when clay images of Mahadevi and Parvati (representing the good side of the Hindu mother goddess) are worshipped for 15 days by women of all castes. Then, to the accompaniment of thundering drums and blaring brass instruments, the images are carried in enormous processions to be immersed in holy waters.

For all its stubborn resistance to Islam, Rajasthan boasts one of India's most religiously tolerant societies. Hindus and Muslims regularly join in each other's festivals and holy celebrations. Also, one of the holiest Muslim shrines in India the tomb of the Sufi mystic Kwajah Mu'in-ud-Din Christi is located at Ajmer. Some 300,000 Muslims from all over the world gather there on the anniversary of the saint's death. It was here, in the 12th century, that Islam achieved its first success in penetrating Rajasthan and in establishing some religious authority. Today, it is a testament to an enduring tolerance— one of which the Rajasthanis deserve to be proud.

Far Left: The Gangor festival of Rajasthan celebrates the Hindu mother goddess.
Left: One of the many spectacular buildings that fill the landscape of Rajasthan.

Traditional arts and crafts, as well as festivals, are a large part of the culture in this important region of India.

The South

Kathakali

What is the most visually stunning thing about Kathakali? The movement? The masks? The décor? It is hard to say.

Kathakali is an art form unique to southern India, and more specifically to the state of Kerala, where it has become emblematic of an entire culture.

It is theatre, mime, dance, music, and art all at once. It is a living, breathing, evolving culture close to the heart of Keralans.

The elements of Kathakali are many and varied: makeup, costumes, drama, music, literature, and dance. The aim is to create a harmonious unity out of them all.

The subject of the dances usually derives from the great Hindu mythological epics, the *Ramayana* and the *Mahabharata*. The action usually takes place outside, and can continue for an entire night.

The players are normally all male, with men and boys taking on female roles. To this end, the costumes worn by Kathakali performers are often very elaborate, with special care given to the carving and crafting of headdresses. Applying makeup, or *chutty*, is another painstaking operation, which is performed by specially trained artists using crude mixtures of lime, coconut, rice paste, indigo, and amorphous sulphur.

The human voice has a central role in Kathakali, a bit like the chorus in ancient Greek dramas. The legends are chanted, and the characters mime the action, all to the accompaniment of a bewildering array of percussions. The most heavily featured drums are beaten with sticks (*chendai*), finger drums (*maddalam*), gongs (*chendila*), and cymbals (*illathalam*). This array of instruments can produce sounds ranging from the murmur of the breeze to the mightiest of thunderclaps.

It is probably the dancing that most visitors remember from Kathakali. It is physical sometimes brutally so and exhausting for the performers, although it is usually reserved for intervals between the vocal chants that tell the story. Gestures are elaborate and stylized; facial expressions even more so. Some kathakali masters are so skilled, having trained their facial muscles to such a high degree, that they can laugh with one side of their face while crying with the other. Tiny gestures, such as the pointing of an accusing finger, can be followed by the wild movements of flailing arms. Given the weight of the headdresses, not to mention frequently outlandish costumes of skirts, necklaces, garlands, and trinkets and the length of the performance, it can be a tiring business. Little wonder that one of the characteristic stances of the kathakali dancer is a bowlegged one, with feet turned inward. It prevents sore feet!

Far Left: Dances that depict mythical Hindu epics are typical of the southern region of Kerala.

Left: Mime, dance, theater, and masks are all typical of the southern regions of India.

The South

Fishermen

India's gigantic coastline means that its fishing industry is large. Indeed, there have even been disputes between Pakistan and India over fishing rights in the northeastern Arabian Sea, off the coast of Gujarat state. India enjoys fishing territories that stretch 200 miles (322 km) out from the northern and eastern coasts into the Indian Ocean. But it is with the south of India, rather than the north, that the image of Indian fishing is perhaps most associated. Barefoot boys splashing into the surf from golden beaches, and venerable old fishermen hauling in nets at sunset, as the surf laps around their ramshackle boats. The exotic hauls of shark, marlin, and sailfish, and the little communities living in stilt houses and houseboats who live off fresh- and seawater fishing in the hot and humid states of Kerala and Tamil Nadu. While India does have a large fishing fleet, the vast majority of the boats operated by India's five million fishermen are creaky but trusty vessels powered by sail or oars, and Kerala is where many of the most picturesque boats are to be found. These are often canoe-shaped, with the bows pointing upwards (sometimes a little Hindu shrine is placed there). The fishermen trawl the waters dressed in a sari-like skirt called a *lunghi*, and, like their ancestors, they fish with a homemade, half-mile (805 m) net called a *seine*. Often, the skippers of these boats are part-timers—although sometimes the boats carry just a single fisherman.

But even here, in one of India's poorest and most traditional regions, things are changing. The Indian government now offers subsidies to fishermen to pay for them to motorize their vessels, and other developments indicate that many of these men—who employ centuries-old methods handed down from father to son—are seeing their lives altered.

Incredibly, the cell phone is one of the devices that a traditional fisherman can use to make a better living. Millions of Indians now use cell phones, and fishermen have found them useful too. While out at sea, they can call onshore dealers and describe the size and quality of their catch, which enables them to find the best price for it.

The poorest fishermen are no longer forced to take the first price offered for the catch, which they had to do out of fear of the catch rotting in the quayside sunshine. Now they can organize a price by phone while far from port. The catch can be almost anything, so rich and varied are the waters off Kerala—eels, sardines, oysters, and rays. Much of this is transported all over India or to Japan, and prices are rising. But many fishermen still save some of the catch for their own meals at home. This is one tradition of the southern Indian sea that will not change any time soon.

Right: Fishing remains an important industry in Kerala.
Far Right: Collecting grass from the bottom of a lake in Kashmir. Boats are one of many useful agricultural tools of India.

In places like Goa, where the weather remains warm all year round, waterways are an important feature of life and of the landscape.

The East

The far eastern region of India is almost a separate country or it could be many different countries. North and east of Kolkata and Bengal lie a series of unique and remote states. Some, like the little kingdom of Sikkim, nestled in the Himalayan river valleys, have almost complete autonomy from the Delhi government. This is where cultural traditions, tribes, religious beliefs, music, art, and food differ greatly from the subcontinent as a whole. It is where India seems most fragmented. All regions and states in the subcontinent are different, but here it seems they are more individual than most. Even the weather is distinctive. This is, one could say, India's Wild East.

Outside Sikkim, there are seven states in the region, and they are known as the Seven Sisters. The eastern states share only a 13-mile (21 km) long border with India a tiny, jagged ribbon of land known as the Chicken's Neck. The Seven Sisters are Arunachal Pradesh, Assam, Manipur, Meghalaya, Mizoram, Nagaland, and Tripura.

The region was also the location of the short Indo-Chinese war of 1962. The secession of another eastern province, Bangladesh, in the war of 1971 emphasized how isolated this region is from the teeming and bustling centers of Indian state power. Even now, it is poor, transport links are insufficient, and unemployment is high. But its peoples are proud of their independence, both from Delhi and from each other.

Assam, so famous for its teas and sugar, is populated by Indo-Iranians and other peoples from further east in Asia. They speak a language called Assamese, but there are also 44 minority languages. For centuries, it is believed to have been a capital of sun worship and astrology, and experts believe that the Surya Pahar temple was a center for these practices.

While Assam is poor but mysterious, Arunachal Pradesh is a natural haven for tourists. It has the great River Brahmaputra, cutting canyons through its foggily forested jungle slopes. But it also has an animistic belief system, practiced by the Mongol people, which reminds the visitor that the borders with Myanmar (Burma) and China are close by. Tribal relations are strong here, with many peoples like the Adis and Nishis having brought their customs from Tibet and the ancient mountain autocracy of Bhutan. Buddhism is secondary to planetary worship and animism, whose origins like the rituals and images that accompany it are lost in the mists of time.

The sensitive border region of Manipur is even more ethnically diverse. Despite a tiny population, it boasts 30 different ethnic groups from all over southern Asia. Meithi, almost never heard anywhere else in India, is the state language. It is, however, a very beautiful region, riddled with lovely wooded canyons. The British aristocrat Lord Irwin described it as "the Switzerland of India." In return, Manipur gave the British Empire the game of polo. The bizarre martial arts of Sarit Sarak and Thang Ta also have their roots here, and the region is known in the rest of the subcontinent for the refined, slow-motion folk dance known as Ras Lila.

Cambodia's Khmer language appears in certain tribal regions in Meghalaya, as does a very unusual law unusual for India: a widow inherits their husband's estate on his death, not his sons. It is also unique on the subcontinent for being India's wettest state, with 47.2 inches (1200 mm) of rain falling every year, leading their muddy rivers to flood.

The same geography can be found in the state of Mizoram, which borders Myanmar. Most strangely, despite the fact that the majority Mizo tribe probably migrated many centuries ago from China, 87 percent of them practice Christianity. A smaller tribe, the Chakma, believe in a fusion of Buddhism, Hinduism, and Animism. Some Mizos have, in the last decades, been converting to Judaism. Mizoram is poor, but quickly growing into one of the most dynamic of the eastern frontier states. With great reserves of limestone and having 30 percent of its territory covered in bamboo forest, hopes are high. As they are for the development of a tourist industry, given the scenic beauty and the great variety of faiths and cultural traditions on offer to the curious and adventurous traveler. Meghalaya may have the gently seductive Ras Lila, but Mizoram has the energetic ritual of the Bamboo Dance, which is performed with bamboo staves to wish the dead a safe trip to the afterlife.

Christianity is also for the main religion of Nagaland, a region populated by a Tibeto-Burmese tribe. According to scriptures, they were once headhunters, and today, because of the many spoken dialects, they still lack a common written language. Nagas are also known for their unique specialty of intricately woven textiles, which are turned into anything from tablemats and shawls to bamboo curtains all of the highest craftsmanship.

Tripura is unusual in that, despite the fact that high mountains can be seen in the distance from almost anywhere, it consists largely of low-lying and swampy land with dense jungles. Sugar is grown in abundance, and very fine it is too. Improvised dances on religious observance days (most Tripuris are Hindu) include the agile Hojagiri dance, which involves the delicate art of balancing on a water-pitcher.

A journey on the rough roads through the Chicken's Neck is to escape the reds, browns, and yellows of the subcontinent. Here is a world of every shade of green, white curtains of rain, white crowns on distant rust-colored peaks, and the indescribable sparkle of tribal finery. It is a reminder that here one is on the threshold of a whole new world of wonders.

Right: As with many regions in India, the colorful statues, rituals, and festivals are emblematic of the religious zeal of the people.

Sadhus

Holy Men of India

Bottom Left: Often naked, with painted bodies, the Sadhus are one of the oldest monastic traditions on earth.

Center: Most Sadhus live a life of prayer and meditation.

Right: Sadhus are considered the holiest men of the Hindu religion.

Sadhus and they are not always men are among the holiest figures in Hinduism. Their practices are believed to date back to 1500 BC, making them the oldest monastic tradition on earth.

They are ascetics, who practice self-denial and the ancient philosophy of yoga. They have given up the pursuit of pleasure, wealth, and duty to serve their religion. Often living as hermits in caves or forests, they can sometimes be found in Hindu temples.

Their name comes from the Sanskrit word for meditation, or *sadhana*. Despite the severity and hardship of their lives, the five million sadhus practicing in India today command fear and respect. They are referred to by most people by the term *baba*, meaning father or mentor.

There are many colorful stories about the extreme lengths to which some sadhu sects go to prove their faith. Some live in cemeteries to talk to ghosts; others, like the famous *nagas*, walk around naked. Then there are the *jata*, who carry swords. Perhaps the most notable sadhu is the one who was entered in the *Guinness Book of World Records* for having remained standing for 17 years. Most sadhus live quietly in contemplation and prayer,

however. Many even live in cities, although they remain in the quiet seclusion of communities called *ashrams*.

Most are men, who enter the practice in their teens or early twenties, often to escape hardship or family difficulties. It is hardly an easy life being a sadhu, as their poverty is often relieved only by the goodwill and donation of alms by ordinary people. There are a few female sadhus named Sadvhis, who worship the goddess Devi from small ascetic communities.

Sadhus are legally declared dead in India and, bizarrely, have to attend their own funerals before beginning to study with a guru and taking up one of the two main branches of sadhu worship, that of the gods Shiva or Vishnu.

Most sadhus, in particular the perpetual pilgrim sadhus, can be seen trudging along the roads of India in service of their god. Every six years, millions of sadhus can be found at the grand festival of Kumbh Mela—the largest human gathering in the world—when they assemble at various points on the banks of the Ganges to bathe and be purified in its holy waters.

For many, India is a source of inspiration and devotion. A place of tranquil beauty, it is home to one of the most colorful, vibrant cultures on earth.

Useful Information

General:

India Tourism Office, USA
Address: 3550 Wilshire Boulevard Suite 204
Los Angeles, CA 90010-2485
Tel: (213) 380-8855
Fax: (213) 380-6111
Email: goitola@aol.com

Ministry of Tourism, India
Address: Transport Bhavan, Parliament Street,
New Delhi 110 001,
Tel: +91 23711995. Fax: +91 23710518.
Email: contactus@incredibleindia.org
Website: www.incredibleindia.org

www.thebestofindia.com
thebestofindia.com is an online encyclopedia and directory offering extensive information about India and its unique culture.

Indian Art and Performing Arts:

Indira Gandhi National Centre for the Arts
Address: 1, C. V. Mess
Janpath
New Delhi 110 001
India
Website: www.ignca.nic.in
This center offers exhibitions on a wide spectrum of encompassing subjects from archaeology to dance and anthropology to photographic art.

ITC Sangeet Research Academy
Address: 1, Netaji Subash Chandra Bose Road
Tollygunge
Kolkata 700 040
India
Website: www.itcsra.org/sra_index/sra_index.html
ITC-SRA was established in 1978 with the objective of preserving and promoting Hindustani Classical Music.

Development:

United Nations Development Programme (UNDP)
Address: 55 Lodhi Estate
Post Box No. 3059
New Delhi - 110 003
India
Website: www.undp.org.in
The United Nations Development Programme (UNDP) and its predecessor organizations have been actively involved in supporting the national development priorities of India for the last five decades.

Geography:

Bombay Natural History Society
Address: Hornbill House
Shaheed Bhagat Singh Road
Mumbai 400 023
India
Website: www.bnhs.org
The Bombay Natural History Society is the largest non-governmental organization (NGO) in the Indian subcontinent engaged in nature conservation research.

WWF India
Address: 172-B Lodi Road
New Delhi 110 003
India
Website: www.wwfindia.org
WWF's India website provides details of upcoming and ongoing projects in climate change, species protection and sustainable living, taking place across the subcontinent region.

Indian History:

www.sscnet.ucla.edu/southasia/History/mainhist.html
A rich resource on the history, sociocultural and political aspects of India.

www.fordham.edu/halsall/india/indiasbook.html
Internet Indian History Sourcebook is a compilation of texts derived from three major online sourcebooks and references. It provides information on every aspect of Indian history.

Indian News and Media:

Web addresses for India's English-language national newspapers:
www.hinduonnet.com
www.hindustantimes.in
www.timesofindia.indiatimes.com

Doordarshan is India's national public TV broadcaster.
www.ddindia.gov.in/

All India Radio is India's national radio network.
www.allindiaradio.org/

Religion:

www.asianinfo.org
Includes a full listing of the various religions prevalent in India.

www.culturalindia.net
Gives extensive information about India's religious diversity and also includes details about the role of pilgrimage in modern-day India.

Indian Medicine—Ayurveda:

The Association of Ayurvedic Professionals of North America
Website: www.aapna.com/
The AAAPNA was formed in 2003; all its practitioners have studied ayurveda in India and aim to share Ayurvedic knowledge and wisdom with health professionals and the general public in North America.

Central Council of Indian Medicine
Address: Jawahar Lal Nehru Bhartiya Chikitsa Avam
Homoeopathy Anusandhan Bhawan
61-65, Institutional Area,
Janakpuri,
New Delhi 110058
India
Website: www.ccimindia.org
The Central Council of Indian Medicine is a regulatory body for several Indian Systems of Medicine including Ayurved, Siddha and Unani Tibb and gives detailed information about training.

Index